SOLDIER A: SAS

BEHIND IRAQI LINES

SOLDIER A: SAS

BEHIND IRAQI LINES

Shaun Clarke

First published in Great Britain 1993
22 Books, 2 Soho Square, London W1V 5DE

Copyright © 1993 by Shaun Clarke

The moral right of the author has been asserted

A CIP catalogue record for this book is available from the
British Library

ISBN 1 898125 00 7

Typeset by Hewer Text Composition Services, Edinburgh
Printed in Great Britain by Cox and Wyman Ltd, Reading

7 9 10 8 6

PRELUDE

Just after two in the morning the Kuwaiti Customs and Immigration officials playing cards at a table in the concrete administration office of the Al-Abdaly checkpoint were distracted by a rumbling sound approaching from the border of Iraq. Lowering their cards and removing their cigarettes from their lips, they glanced quizzically at one another as other officials, who had been dozing at their desks, were awakened by the increasing noise.

The floor began shaking beneath the men's feet. At first bewildered, then slowly realizing that the unthinkable might be happening, the senior official, an overfed, jowly man in a dusty, tattered uniform, dropped his cards onto the table, stood up and walked to the door. By the time he opened it, the whole building was shaking and the distant rumbling was rapidly drawing nearer.

1

The Customs official looked out of the doorway as the first of a convoy of 350 Iraqi tanks smashed through the wooden barriers of the checkpoint. Shocked almost witless, he dropped his cigarette and stared in disbelief as one tank after another rumbled past, noisily smashing the rest of the barrier and sending pieces of wood flying everywhere.

Fear welled up in the official when he saw shadowy figures in the billowing clouds of dust created by the tanks. Realizing that they were armed troops advancing between the tanks, he slammed the door shut, bawled a warning to his colleagues, then raced back to his desk to make a hurried telephone call to Kuwait City, informing his superiors of what was happening.

He was still talking when the rapid fire of a Kalashnikov AK47 assault rifle blew the lock off the door, allowing it to be violently kicked open. Iraqi troops rushed in to rake the room with their weapons, massacring all those inside and – more important from their point of view – blowing the telephones to pieces.

As the spearhead of Saddam Hussein's military machine rumbled along the 50-mile, six-lane highway leading to Kuwait City, troops were dropped off at every intersection to capture Kuwaitis entering or leaving. Other troops disengaged from the main convoy to drag stunned Kuwaiti truck drivers from their vehicles and either shoot them on the spot or, if they were lucky, keep them prisoner at gunpoint.

Simultaneously, Iraqi special forces, airlifted in by helicopter gunships, were parachuting from the early-morning sky to secure road junctions, government buildings, military establishments and other key positions in the sleeping capital.

Moving in on the city, still out of earshot of most of those sleeping, were a million Iraqi troops, equipped with hundreds of artillery pieces, multiple-rocket launchers, and a wide variety of small arms. Stretched out along a 200-mile front, obscured by clouds of dust created by Saddam Hussein's five and a half thousand battle tanks, they endured because they were motivated by months of starvation and their growing envy of Kuwaiti wealth.

In air-conditioned hotels, marble-walled boudoirs and lushly carpeted official residences, the citizens of Kuwait were awakened by the sound of aircraft and gunfire from the outskirts of the city. Wondering what was happening, they tuned in to Kuwait Radio and heard emergency broadcasts from the Ministry of Defence, imploring the Iraqi aggressors to cease their irresponsible attack or face the consequences. Those who heard the broadcasts, Kuwaitis and foreigners alike, went to their windows and looked out in disbelief as parachutists glided down against a backdrop of distant, silvery explosions and beautiful webbed lines of crimson tracers. It all seemed like a dream.

Thirty minutes later, as the early dawn broke with the light of a blood-red sun, the grounds of the Dasman Palace were being pounded by the rocket fire of the Iraqis' Russian-built MiG fighters. Even as the Emir of Kuwait was being lifted off by a helicopter bound for Saudia Arabia, his Royal Guard, pitifully outnumbered, were being cut down by Iraqi tanks and stormtroopers. In addition, the Emir's half-brother, Sheikh Fahd, who had nobly refused to leave, had been fatally wounded on the steps of the palace.

While Hussein's tanks surrounded the British and American embassies, his jets were rocket-bombing the city's airport, illuminating the starlit sky with jagged flashes of silver fire, which soon turned into billowing black smoke. Two guards died as Iraqi troops burst into Kuwait's Central

Bank to begin what would become an orgy of looting.

By dawn the Iraqis were in control of key military installations and government buildings in the capital, Kuwait's pocket army was fighting a losing battle to protect the invaluable Rumaila oilfields and thousands of wealthy Kuwaitis and expatriate Britons, Americans, Europeans and Russians, trying to flee to Saudi Arabia, were being turned back by the Iraqi tanks and troops encircling the city.

Having returned to their homes, the expatriates heard their embassies advise them on the radio to stock up with food and stay indoors. Those brave enough to venture out to replenish their food stocks saw Iraqi generals riding around in confiscated Mercedes while their troops, long envious of Kuwaiti prosperity, machine-gunned the windows of the stores in Fahd Salem Street, joining the growing numbers of looters. Soon reports of rape were spreading throughout the city.

Before sunset, the invaders had dissolved Kuwait's National Assembly, shut ports and airports, imposed an indefinite curfew and denounced the absent Emir and his followers as traitorous agents of the Jews and unspecified foreign powers.

No mention was made of the Iraqi tanks burning in the grounds of the fiercely defended Dasman Palace, the sporadic gunfire still heard throughout the city as loyal Kuwaitis sniped at the invaders or the many dead littering the streets.

Even as the sun was sinking, torture chambers were being set up all over the city and summary executions, by shotgun or hanging, were becoming commonplace.

By midnight, Kuwait as the world knew it had ceased to exist; the armoured brigades of the Middle East's most feared tyrant stood at the doors of Saudi Arabia; and thousands of foreigners, including Britons, were locked in hotels or in their homes, cowering under relentless shellfire or hiding in basements, attics, cupboards and water tanks as Iraqi troops, deliberately deprived of too much for too long, embarked on an orgy of looting, torture, rape, murder and mindless destruction.

1

On 1 January 1991, almost four months to the day after Saddam Hussein's bloody take-over of Kuwait City, an RAF C-130 Hercules transport plane secretly took off from RAF Brize Norton, Oxfordshire. It was transporting members of the SAS (Special Air Service) and the SBS (Special Boat Squadron) to a holding area in Riyadh – the joint capital, with Jeddah, of Saudi Arabia – located in the middle of the country and surrounded by desert.

Though the SAS men were pleased to be back in business, the fact that they had been called back to their Hereford base on Boxing Day, when most of them were at home celebrating with family or friends, had caused some of them to voice a few complaints. Now, as they sat in cramped conditions, packed in like sardines with their weapons, bergens, or backpacks, and other equipment in the gloomy, noisy hold of the Hercules, some of them were passing the time by airing the same gripes.

'My missus was fucking mad,' Corporal Roy 'Geordie' Butler told his friends, in a manner that implied he agreed with her. 'No question about it. Her whole family was there, all wearing their best clothes, and she was just putting the roast in the oven when the telephone rang. When I told her I'd been called back to Hereford and had to leave right away, she came out with a mouthful of abuse that made her family turn white. They're all Christian, her side.'

'Don't sound so hard done by, Geordie,' said Corporal 'Taff' Burgess. 'We can do without that bullshit. We all know your heart was broken a few years back when your missus, after leaving you for a month, returned home to make your life misery. You were having a great time without her in the pubs in Newcastle.'

That got a laugh from the others. 'Hear, hear!' added Jock McGregor. 'Geordie probably *arranged* the phone calls to get away from his missus and her family. Come on, Geordie, admit it.'

'Go screw yourself, Sarge'. She's not bad, my missus. Just because she made a mistake in the past, doesn't mean she's no good. Forgive and forget, I say. I just think they could have picked another day. Boxing Day, for Christ's sake!'

But in truth, he'd been relieved. Geordie was a tough nut and he couldn't stand being at home. He didn't mind his wife – who had, after all, only left him for a month to go and moan about him to her mother in Gateshead – but he couldn't stand domesticity, the daily routine in Newcastle – doing the garden, pottering about the house, watching telly, walking the dog, slipping out for the odd pint – it was so bloody boring. No, he needed to be with the Regiment, even if it meant being stuck in Hereford, doing nothing but endless retraining and field exercises. And now, with some real work to do, he felt a lot happier.

'What about you, Danny?' Geordie asked Corporal 'Baby Face' Porter. 'What about your missus? How did she take it?'

'Oh, all right,' Danny answered. He was a man of few words. 'She understood, I suppose.'

'I'll *bet* she did,' Corporal Paddy Clarke said.

Sergeant-Major Phil Ricketts smiled, but kept his mouth shut. He knew Danny's wife, Darlene, and didn't think much of her. Danny had married her eight years earlier, just after the Falklands war. Having once spent a weekend leave with Danny and his parents in the Midlands, a few weeks before Danny proposed to his Darlene, Ricketts felt that he knew where Danny was coming from. Always intrigued by the contradiction between Danny's professional killer's instincts and his naïvety about personal matters, he had not been surprised to find that Darlene's father was a drunken loudmouth, her mother a tart and Darlene pretty much like her mother.

Nevertheless, blinded by love, Danny had married Darlene and was now the proud father of two children: a boy and a girl, seven and six respectively. While Danny had never been one for talking much, it was becoming increasingly evident from his unease at the very mention of Darlene's name that he was troubled by secret doubts which he could not articulate. The marriage, Ricketts suspected, was on the rocks and Danny didn't want to even think about it.

No such problem, however, with the big black sergeant, Andrew Winston, formerly of Barbados, who was sitting beside Danny, looking twice his size, and crafting poetry in his notebook, as he usually did to pass the time. In fact, since the Falklands campaign, Andrew had become something of a celebrity within the Regiment, having had his first book of poems published by a small company based in London's Notting Hill Gate, and even receiving a good review in the highly respected magazine *Orbit*. When most of the book's print-run was remaindered, Andrew bought the books himself, and sold them off cheaply, personally signed, either to his friends in the Regiment or, more often, to their wives, who clearly were deeply interested in six-foot, handsome, black poets.

As the poems were about Andrew's experiences with the Regiment, he had also sent copies of the book to the Imperial War Museum. When the curator wrote back, thanking him for his contribution and assuring him that the three signed copies would be placed in the museum's library, Andrew was so thrilled that he rushed straight out and married his latest girlfriend, a beauty from his home town in Barbados. Now he too was a father – in his case, of three girls – and he appeared to have no complaints.

'I used to spend so much time chasing nooky,' he explained to Ricketts, 'that I didn't have any left for my poetry. Now I've got it on tap every night and I'm much more creative. Marriage has its good points, Sarge.'

In the intervening years, Ricketts had been

promoted to sergeant-major, Andrew to corporal and then sergeant, while Jock McGregor, Paddy Clarke and the reticent Danny had become corporals. Geordie Butler and Taff Burgess, however, although experienced soldiers, had repeatedly been denied promotion because of their many drunken misdemeanours. Also because, as Ricketts suspected, they simply didn't want responsibility and *preferred* being troopers.

As for Ricketts, now nearing 40, he was increasingly fond of the comforts of home, appreciating his wife Maggie more than ever, and taking a greater interest in his two daughters. It still surprised him that they were now virtually adults: Anna, 19, was working as a hairdresser in Hereford, while Julia, a year younger, was preparing to take her A levels and hoping to go to art school. Though he was proud of them, they made him feel his age.

Now, thinking about his family, and surrounded by his men in the cramped, clamorous hold of the Hercules, Ricketts was forced to countenance the fact that the battle for Kuwait might be his last active engagement with the Regiment. In future, while still being involved, he was more likely to be in the background, planning and orchestrating ops, rather than taking part in them. For that reason, he was looking forward to this campaign with even more enthusiasm than usual. It marked a specific stage in his life, and a very important one. After this he would settle down.

'How much longer to go?' Andrew asked no one in particular, suffering from a creative block and just needing someone to talk to.

'About twenty minutes,' Ricketts replied. 'We're already descending.'

'Thank Christ,' Andrew burst out. 'I can't stand these damned flights. You can burn me or freeze me or shoot me, man, but keep me out of these transports. I can't bear being cooped up.'

'You're going to be cooped up when we land,' Paddy gloated. 'In a fucking OP in the fucking desert – hot by day, cold by night. How's that grab you, Sergeant?'

'I don't mind,' Andrew replied. 'I'm a man who likes his privacy. Just stick me in a hole in the ground and let me live with myself. Since I'm the only man here worth talking to, I'd rather talk to myself.'

'You might find yourself talking to an Iraqi trying to cut your black throat.'

'Lord have mercy, hallelujah, I is ready and waitin'. Ever since that Saddam Hussein pissed on Kuwait City I's bin dyin' to come to the rescue. It's part of my imperialist nature. My noble English blood, brothers!'

As the customary repartee – bullshit, as they always called it – poured from the other troopers, Ricketts thought of the march of events that had followed Saddam's invasion. When the news broke, Ricketts had been sceptical about Saddam's remaining in Kuwait City, assuming it to be a bluff designed to get him his way in other matters. Since then, however, Saddam had stuck to his guns. Because of his intransigence, the UN had imposed economic sanctions and a trade ban on Iraq; President Bush had 'drawn a line in the sand' and sent thousands of troops to Saudi Arabia; 12 Arab states, along with Britain and France, had done the same; over 100,000 refugees had crossed into Jordan; Saddam had used British hostages as a 'human shield', paraded others on television, and then declared Kuwait Iraq's nineteenth province and released the hostages as a political gesture; and the UN Security Council had voted for the use of force against Iraq if it did not withdraw from Kuwait by 15 January.

By 22 December, shortly after the UN General Assembly had condemned Iraq for violating human rights in Kuwait, Saddam had vowed that he would never give up Kuwait and threatened to use atomic and chemical weapons if attacked. As he was still showing no signs of relenting, war was almost certainly on the cards.

''Scuse me for asking, boss,' Geordie said to Major Hailsham, 'but is it true we're not the first to be flown in?'

'I don't know what you're talking about,' Major Hailsham replied. He had been promoted shortly after his return from the Falklands, when Major Parkinson was transferred to another unit. With his sardonic sense of humour and excellent operational record, he was a popular commanding officer of the squadron.

'You don't?'

'No, Trooper, I don't. If any other members of the Regiment have been inserted, I wasn't informed.' Mike Hailsham was still a handsome schoolboy with a wicked grin. 'But since I'm only the CO of *this* benighted squadron, they wouldn't even *think* to inform me, would they?'

'I guess that's right, boss,' Geordie responded, deadpan. 'We'll all have to accept that.'

In truth they all knew, and were envious of the fact, that other members of the Regiment had been working undercover in Iraq since a few days before the invasion, having flown incognito, in 'civvies', on British Airways flight 149 from London to Delhi, with a fuelling stop in Kuwait. Finding themselves in the middle of Saddam's invasion, which had begun in the middle of that same morning – slightly earlier than anticipated by the 'green slime', the Intelligence Corps – the SAS men had melted away, dispersing in two directions, some to send back information from behind Iraqi lines, others to do the same from Kuwait itself, where they would now be hiding in a succession of 'safe' houses and operating under the very noses of the Iraqis. Naturally, their presence in Kuwait was unofficial and therefore remained resolutely unacknowledged.

'We're coming in to land.' Hailsham observed needlessly as the overloaded Hercules began its shuddering descent. 'Check your kit and prepare to disembark. I want no delays.'

'Aye, aye, boss,' Ricketts said, then bawled the same order along the hold of the aircraft.

Cumbersome at the best of times, though always reliable, the Hercules shuddered even more as it descended, groaning and squealing as if about to fall apart. Eventually it bounced heavily onto the runway, bellowed, shook violently and rattled as it taxied along the tarmac, before finally groaning to a halt.

Letting out a united cheer, the men unsnapped their safety belts and stood up in a tangle of colliding weapons and bergens. After a lot of noise from outside, the transport's rear ramp fell down, letting light pour in, and the men clattered down onto the sunlit, sweltering tarmac of Riyadh airport.

It was not the end of the SAS men's long journey. Lined up along the runway of the airport were RAF Tornado F-3 air-defence aircraft which had arrived four months ago, shortly after the fall of Kuwait, flying in from the massive Dhahran air-base. There were also a dozen RAF CH-47 Chinook helicopters of 7 Squadron's Special Forces Flight.

The Regiment's recently acquired, state-of-the-art desert warfare weaponry, including Thorn-EMI 5kg hand-held thermal imagers, Magellan satellite navigation aids – SATNAV GPS, or Global Positioning Systems – laser designators and other equipment, was unloaded from the Hercules and transferred to the Chinooks. When the transfer was over, the men, who had been milling about on the tarmac, stretching their legs and breathing in deeply the warm, fresh air, also boarded the helicopters and were flown on to Al Jubail, an immense, modern port on Saudi Arabia's east coast, some four hundred miles from Riyadh and about five hundred from Kuwait City. They emerged from the Chinooks a couple of hours later, glad to be back on solid ground.

Though originally built as a centre for oil and light industry, Al Jubail had never been developed properly and was now being used fully for the first time as a receiving port for the Allied equipment and supplies being brought in on more than a hundred ships, mostly from European ports, but also from Cyprus, Liberia and Panama. While some of the British servicemen in transit, mainly those of the Queen's Royal Irish Hussars and the 7th Armoured Brigade, were billeted in huts and sheds originally intended for the industrial workers, most were housed in the enormous, constantly growing 'Tent City' located in the port area and already equipped with camp-beds, showers, chemical toilets and a field kitchen run by the Americans.

'Home sweet home!' Sergeant Andrew Winston said, dumping his bergen on the floor beside a camp-bed in the sweltering late-afternoon heat of the space allocated to the Regiment for the duration of its stay in Al Jubail.

'Having just come down from the trees,' Geordie replied, 'you'd be used to living out in the open. That's one up to you, Sarge.'

'You don't like it, Geordie? Too hot for you, is it?'

'You could obviously do with sweating off a few pounds,' Geordie replied, tugging experimentally at the ropes of his lean-to tent to check that they were tight, 'but me, I'm as slim as a man can go, so I don't need melting down in this fucking heat.'

'I'm relieved,' Taff Burgess said, laying his M16 out carefully on his camp-bed and gazing out over the rows of tents divided by paths that led in one direction to the port and in the other to the airstrip, other accommodations and the guarded compounds containing the armoured transport and tanks. Hundreds of thousands of troops, British, American and French, crowded the spaces between the tents, eating, drinking, writing letters, taking open-air showers and going in and out of chemical latrines. Their constant movement and the ever-present desert wind created drifting clouds of sand and dust that made them look ghostlike in the shimmering light.

19

'I wouldn't fancy being in one of those huts in this fucking heat,' Taff said. 'It must be like a Turkish bath in there. At least we can breathe out here.'

'All *I'm* breathin' is dust,' replied Jock. 'That and bloody sand. I've got sand in my boots, in my eyes, in my mouth, and even up the eye of my fucking dick. This place is just like Oman.'

'You're too old to remember Oman,' Paddy ribbed him, stretched out languidly on his camp-bed, hands folded beneath his head, acting really cool in the sweltering heat. 'Relax, boys, you're gonna have a good time here. Compared to what's to come, it's probably Paradise.'

'I doubt that,' Geordie said.

He was right. Their accommodations were close to the Royal Corps of Transport's Force Maintenance Area, or FMA, and the constant noise, combined with the heat, made for irritable days and sleepless nights. Since they were there for five days, waiting for the rest of their equipment to be brought in by ship, the lack of sleep was no joke. To make matters worse, they were ordered to take NAP tablets, which were meant to reduce the damaging effects of gas in the event of a chemical attack, but also gave everyone diarrhoea.

'My shit comes out like piss,' Paddy informed the others. 'And I hear these tablets also contain a lot of bromide, so say goodbye to your sex life.'

Already running non-stop to the latrines, they felt even worse after the biological vaccinations against whooping cough, which they received at the same time and which knocked most of them out for twenty-four hours.

'Say goodbye to your fucking sanity,' Jock said groggily, as the others moaned and groaned on their camp-beds. 'Christ, I feel dizzy!'

Scarcely recovered, they were nevertheless made to spend a large part of each day on the Jerboa Range of the training ground at Al Fadhili, inland from Al Jubail, where they shot at targets and markers while being bellowed and spat at by the aggressive camels of passing Bedouin.

'Those bastards on camels are straight out of *Lawrence of Arabia*,' Geordie announced to all within earshot. 'A fucking good film, that was.'

'I never wanted to be in the movies,' Andrew replied, 'and those camels stink. What the hell are we *doing* here?'

'Waiting for the rest of our equipment, coming in with the Navy. Need I say more?'

'Fucking Navy!' Taff spat.

21

Soon sickened by the repetitive, useless training, which they had done many times before,
they were all pleased when, on the fifth day, the
despised Navy finally arrived at the port with
their missing supplies.

By this time, with over half a million Coalition
troops and the greatest air force ever assembled
in history clogging Al Jubail, the space being
used by the SAS was desperately needed. The
Regiment was therefore hurriedly packed up
and driven back to the airstrip. From there,
Hercules transports flew the relieved men to a
forward operating base, or FOB, located at a
Saudi airport in the desert, a day's drive from
the border of western Iraq.

'We operate from here,' Major Hailsham told
the men the minute they stepped off the planes
into another sea of flapping tents on a flat, barren
plain. 'Welcome to hell.'

It wasn't quite hell, but it was certainly no
paradise. The FOB was a dense throng of lean-to
tents divided by roads filled with brightly painted
'Pink Panther' Land Rovers, Honda motorcycles, Challenger tanks, and other armoured
vehicles and trucks, many of which were being
used to support the tents and their camouflaged

netting. On all sides of the makeshift camp there was nothing but desert, stretching nine hundred miles from the Red Sea to Kuwait and the Gulf, southwards to the Arabian Sea beyond Oman – more than a million square miles in all. It was a very big area to cover. Also, it was surprisingly cold, especially at night.

The first thing the SAS men learnt was that they could not phone home, their mail would be censored and normal radio transmissions were restricted. And, of course, they could not drink alcohol – not even here in the desert, for the Bedouin still often passed the camp on their camels. Similarly, the men had to respect Muslim customs and not flaunt their Western habits or religious preferences, except in the privacy of their tents.

'Should this make you resent the fact that we're here to defend the Kuwaitis,' Hailsham said, 'I would remind you that we have our own interests at heart. In fact, we're here to safeguard Arabian oil, which furnishes over two-thirds of the world's needs, including ours. To lose it to Saddam would have devastating consequences for the West, including Great Britain. I'd also remind you that there are approximately thirty thousand expatriates in Saudi Arabia who need our protection. To give them that, we need the trust of the Bedouin. Please don't forget it.'

In their view, the men were not compensated for such restrictions by being treated like lords. On the contrary, their living conditions were basic, with portable showers, chemical toilets and meals consisting mainly of sausages and baked beans, sometimes curry with rice, spooned up from mess-tins as quickly as possible to stop sand or dust from getting on it, then washed down with hot tea.

The freezing nights were long – about eleven hours of darkness – and the men, stretched out beside their tanks and armoured vehicles or huddled up in their slit trenches, could do little to pass the time other than listen to the restricted programmes of Forces Broadcasting or study the brilliant stars over the flat, featureless, seemingly endless black desert.

From the BBC they learned that back in England Wing-Commander David Farquhar had lost secret documents and a laptop computer containing an outline version of the American war plan. The fact that this news was conveyed by the BBC even before it was known officially to the Coalition Forces in the Gulf caused much sardonic mirth among the men. They also learnt that the Prime Minister, Margaret Thatcher, had been replaced by John Major, whom many thought would not be as supportive of them as had been the Iron Lady.

'Not *my* cup of tea,' Major Hailsham said, summing up the general feeling among the men, 'but at least she always stuck by her guns. She also stuck up for the Special Forces. I don't know that John Major will. This could be a bad blow to us.'

'We'll survive,' Sergeant-Major Ricketts replied.

For the SAS, the first five months of the crisis had been a time of intense frustration. As Britain's leading exponents of desert warfare, they were, by January, the only Regiment without a certain role in any war with Iraq, even though an FOB had been established in the Gulf since August, with D and G Squadrons carrying out intensive exercises in the desolate area of the Rub Al Khali, or the Empty Quarter, testing men and equipment. At that stage, their primary function was supposed to be the rescue of the hostages being used as a human shield by Saddam; but with the release of the hostages in the second week of December, that function had become redundant and left them with no clearly defined role.

'At the moment,' Hailsham explained to Ricketts,

'with the cooperation of the American Special Operations Central Command, we're working hand in glove with the 5th Special Forces Group, the Amphibious Sea Air Land, or SEAL, units, the US Air Force special force and the Psychological Operations and Civil Aid or, to be brief, Psyops and Civaid. Also, since it's perfectly clear that the outcome of any war with Saddam Hussein will be determined by air power, we're boning up on the use of lasers for target designation with the Tornado and similar bombers. Front-line reconnaissance, however, is still under the control of the 5th Special Forces Group and US Marine Corps recon specialists. This isn't raising the spirits of the men to any great heights.'

'Presumably we need the permission of our imposing US Commander-in-Chief, Norman Schwarzkopf, to take a more active role,' said Ricketts.

'Unfortunately, yes – though I have it on the best of authority that General Sir Peter de la Billière, our former SAS commander and now commander of the British forces here in Saudi Arabia, is putting in a good word for us.'

'I should bloody hope so,' Ricketts replied.

'Apart from that we're just twiddling our thumbs.'

'There are worse vices, boss.'

Hailsham grinned. 'Anyway, it's bound to happen soon and I think we should consider our course of action. My view is that we should revert to the kind of campaign David Stirling ran during World War Two – deep-penetration, hit-and-run raids behind enemy lines, destroying their planes on the ground, attacking their lines of communication, ambushing their patrols and causing general disruption and mayhem.'

'In armed Land Rovers.'

'Right. The Pink Panthers. In and out in clouds of dust with all guns firing. Personally, I'd love it.'

'Then let's hope we get to do it,' Ricketts said. 'Come on, boss, let's go for chow.'

They were just about to leave the tent when the telephone rang.

2

'I've called you together,' Major Hailsham addressed the troopers assembled outside his lean-to on the edge of the city of tents spread across the desert plain, 'to tell you that plans for the liberation of Kuwait are already well advanced and the operation's been codenamed "Desert Storm".'

When the men burst into applause and cheering, it hit Hailsham just how frustrated they had been during the past few days, not knowing exactly why they were here and fed up with the repetitive lessons on survival in the desert or the use of the latest high-tech equipment. While this FOB was busy and noisy all day, with helicopters constantly taking off and landing, aircraft roaring overhead and Challenger tanks and armoured vehicles being put through their paces, the activity was purely of a time-filling nature, albeit masquerading as practice. Meanwhile, the 'Pink Panther' Land Rovers and motorcycles were sitting idly outside the tents. What Hailsham's men wanted, he now realized, was more positive action and a clearly defined reason for being here. Now at last they were getting it.

'The basic plan,' Hailsham continued when the men had quietened down, 'is for battleships of the US Navy to bombard the Iraqi coastal positions and offshore islands of Kuwait while US Marines make an amphibious landing from the Gulf. At the same time, Arab elements of the Coalition forces will head overland, straight for Kuwait. Meanwhile, US Marine Corps will be engaging the Iraqis due north of them. The Syrians and Egyptians will push to the north, make a right-handed swing, and come into Kuwait City from the west – hopefully, if things go as planned – meeting up with the Coalition Arab forces already there. No Western forces will enter the capital until it's been cleared by Islamic troops.'

'Very decent of us,' Geordie said sarcastically.

'Very sensible of us,' Ricketts pointed out. 'It shows that this war is for the Kuwaitis and we're simply supporting them.'

'Correct,' Hailsham said. 'The city must be liberated by Muslim forces to avoid accusations of exploitation or desecration by Christians. We'll follow them in.'

'So what's the state of play at the moment?' Sergeant Andrew Winston asked. 'Are we ready to move?'

'Not quite. As our heavy tank units haven't arrived yet, all that stands between Saddam's five thousand-odd tanks and the oil riches of Saudi Arabia are a few thousand US paratroopers and Marines . . .' Jeers and farting noises from the SAS troops interrupted Hailsham, who went on, '. . . around twenty-four US Army AH-64A Apache attack helicopters, a few hundred Coalition aircraft, US special Forces Troops . . .' – more derisory remarks and noises from the SAS troopers. – '. . . And, of course, us.' Loud cheering. 'However, while thousands more Coalition troops – British, American and French – are being flown and shipped in every day, the Gulf is filling up with aircraft carriers and their F-18 Hornet fighters, F-14 Tomcat attack fighters, A-6E Intruder bombers, and KA-6d tanker jets for mid-air refuelling. By the time the UN deadline for Saddam's withdrawal is reached, the greatest army in history will have been assembled in Saudi Arabia and will be ready to move.'

'What's our new role,' Danny 'Baby Face'

Porter asked solemnly, 'now that all the hostages have been released?'

'A good question, Corporal. As you're doubtless aware by now, on 2 December Saddam Hussein test-fired three ballistic missiles – similar to the Soviet-built Scuds – over four hundred miles of Iraqi territory, provocatively aiming them in the direction of Israel. It's our belief that if the battle for Kuwait begins – which it will if Saddam ignores the Coalition's demand for withdrawal by the fifteenth of this month – he'll deliberately fire on Israel in order to lure it into the war.'

'So?' Paddy Clarke said. 'We can do with all the help we can get and the Israelis are sharp.'

'I agree about the Israelis, but in this particular theatre of operations we simply can't afford to have them taking part. In fact, their intervention would be an absolute disaster, losing us the Arab members of the Coalition and maybe even turning them against us. Our new task, then, is to help prevent Saddam attacking Israel.'

'And how do we do that?' Jock McGregor asked.

'By locating and destroying the Scud bunkers, trailer-erector launchers, mobile units and support systems hidden deep in Iraqi territory.'

'Can't they be located by satellite?' Andrew Winston asked. 'I've heard that the Yanks have two orbiting spacecraft that can sweep the launch areas with infrared detectors every 12 seconds.'

'They're not all that brilliant,' Sergeant-Major Ricketts pointed out. 'In fact, they even failed to spot Saddam's so-called supergun at Jabe Hamryn, north of Baghdad. That barrel was 170 feet long and sticking into the sky like a big dick – yet the satellites missed it!'

'Ricketts is right,' Major Hailsham said. 'Aerial reconnaissance can be flawed. The recent Scud test shot, from a base near Basra, was in the final stages of its flight before a US satellite detected the flare from its rocket motor. The satellites, it seems, can only pick them up when they're in flight – and that's often too late. Also, the Iraqis are switching off their Squat Eye guidance radar systems, which further reduces our chances of finding them – so we still need good old-fashioned eyeball recces.'

'From OPs.'

'Yes, Corporal Porter, that's the idea.'

'How many Scuds do they have?' Danny asked, as solemn as ever.

'Present estimates vary from four hundred to a thousand missiles on thirty to thirty-six

sites and maybe two hundred mobile launchers.'

Andrew gave a low whistle. 'That's a lot,
boss.'

'No argument there, Sergeant.'

'So what happens when we locate bunkers or
mobile launchers?'

'Either we call in air power or we relay the info
to Intelligence HQ in Riyadh. Patriot surface-to-
air missiles will then be alerted automatically to
the Scud's course and speed – a process that only
takes a few minutes.'

'Our parameters?'

'As of this moment, we're the only ones
allowed to cross the line ahead of other ground
forces.' This caused whistles of approval and sporadic clapping, which tailed off when Hailsham
waved his hand for silence. 'We have a second-
ary reason for being allowed to go in ahead.
The Coalition is greatly concerned about Iraq's
chemical-warfare capability. At the moment we
know very little about the types of chemical
agents Saddam has in his arsenal. We *do* know
he has mustard and nerve gas and is likely to
arm his Scuds with them. So one of our jobs
may be to infiltrate the contaminated areas
and collect samples of the agents being used.

The samples will then be flown back to Porton
Down for analysis and, hopefully, the creation
of an antidote.'

'I don't like the sound of *that*,' Andrew said.
'I don't like them chemicals, man.'

'Nor do I, Sergeant.'

'How do we insert?' Danny asked.

'The Regiment will be broken up into two sets
of mobile teams: one for deep-penetration ops in
Iraq; the other for hit-and-run raids in the desert,
using Land Rovers – just like they did in Africa
during World War Two.'

'Sounds like fun,' Geordie said. 'I'll buy that,
boss.'

'Me, too,' agreed Jock. 'Are you going to throw
in some motorbikes?'

'Yes,' Hailsham said.

'I haven't been in a Pink Panther since Oman,'
Andrew said, glancing back over his shoulder at
the brightly painted Land Rovers and motorcycles on the dusty tracks between the lean-to
tents. 'Look at 'em! As pretty as a picture.' He
turned back to grin at Major Hailsham. 'Count
me in, boss.'

'I have your name and number, Sergeant
Winston.'

'When do we move out?' asked Taff Burgess.

'We have to be gone by the night of the twenty-second. If Saddam doesn't withdraw from Kuwait on the fifteenth, hostilities will begin on the twenty-ninth. That gives us seven days to do as much damage as possible before Desert Storm commences.'

While talking to the men, Hailsham frequently had to shout against the noise of the RAF Chinooks that were taking off and landing in billowing clouds of sand on the nearby airstrip. Even noisier were the Tornado F-3 air-defence planes roaring frequently overhead, going to or returning from practice flights out in the desert. Also churning up clouds of sand and creating a lot of noise were the Challenger tanks being put through their paces on the sands surrounding the camp. This was a large, busy FOB.

'What are the negatives?' Andrew asked.

'Local beliefs, sand and water.'

'That's not too clear, boss.'

'As you know, the men here call the desert the GAFA, or "Great Arabian Fuck All".' The explanation copped a few knowing laughs. 'It's amusing, but accurate,' Hailsham said when the laughter had died down. 'Out there, where we'll be going, the desert appears to be empty of every-thing except sand and gravel. That appearance,

35

however, is deceptive. Even the most barren stretch probably belongs to somebody and will be highly valued as grazing for the camels still maintained here by the Saudis, particularly those of high rank. As it is with their religion, so it is with their property: we have to be careful not to give offence.'

'And the other problems?'

'Too much sand and too little water,' Hailsham replied. 'Sand ingestion gives us severe mechanical problems. Even with filters, the life of helicopter engines is reduced to about a tenth of normal usage. The power-packs of the Challenger tanks are failing so often that 7th Armoured Brigade's desert training had to be curtailed. Other supply vehicles that were perfectly fine in Europe, when loaded here sink into the sand. And container trucks are particularly useless here. In fact, we've had to borrow a lot of M453 tracked vehicles from the Yanks. We'll be using them in conjunction with wheeled vehicles for staged resupply journeys. A further problem is that the desert is mostly flat, featureless terrain, which makes direction-finding difficult for the supply trucks. They can also get bogged down in the sand, thus becoming exposed.'

None of the men showed too much concern at that.

'Water?' Danny asked.

'It normally comes from the desalination plant at Al Jubail, but if we miss the REME supply columns, or if we're out on patrol, we'll have to drink the fossil water from the prehistoric aquifers beneath the desert floor. Of course the sappers will also be prospecting the best sites for artesian wells, but they have to negotiate with local landowners, who aren't always keen.'

'I'd rather drink my own piss,' big Andrew said. 'It won't be the first time.'

'As it is with the flight crewmen,' Hailsham continued when the laughter had died down, 'you'll all be given approximately £800 worth of gold, to help you if you're caught or find yourselves cut off and faced with non-friendly civilians who want their palms greased. You'll also be carrying a chit written in Arabic, promising that Her Majesty's Government will pay the sum of £5000 to anyone who returns you safely to friendly territory or persons. If nothing else, I trust that makes you feel important.'

'I'm important enough without that,' said Andrew without hesitation. 'You can look me up in the Imperial War Museum. I'm in there with the greats.'

'You do us all proud, Sergeant Winston. Any questions, men?'

'Yeah,' Paddy said. 'What do we do between now and the twenty-second?'

'We prepare,' Hailsham said.

The men dispersed and went their separate ways, most of them looking a lot happier than they had done for the past couple of days.

Ricketts put his thumb up in the air. 'Very good, boss.' Hailsham just grinned.

3

On 19 January, five days before the planned date, the Squadron was kitted out with weapons, survival equipment and battle clothes especially modified for desert conditions, before being flown from the FOB to a landing zone (LZ) somewhere deep in Iraq.

Since the briefing in early January, they had all undergone special training and weapons testing in the Empty Quarter, a vast, uninhabited region some distance from Al Jubail, with an emphasis on desert driving, survival in dust, sand, fierce heat and freezing cold, the protection of weapons from the same, and direction-finding by the moon and stars in case of compass failure. They were also trained in the use of laser designators for marking targets. All were looking forward to finishing the training and being airlifted to the LZ on the twenty-second.

They were therefore taken by surprise when, at 0001 hours Zulu – one minute past three local time, or one minute past midnight Greenwich Mean Time – on Thursday 17 January, two days after the deadline given for Saddam's withdrawal from Kuwait – which he ignored – eight US Apaches of the 101st Airborne Division, equipped with laser spot trackers and range-finders, attacked Iraqi radars with Hellfire missiles, rockets and 30mm cannon shells, destroying two command centres and their Soviet radars, Tall Spoon and King Rest, thereby creating a safe corridor for Allied aircraft.

Simultaneously, Tomahawk Cruise missiles from the Coalition aircraft-carriers in the Gulf rained down on Baghdad while British Tornadoes skimmed at low level across the desert at 800kph, also heading north for Baghdad. These were followed almost instantly by another wave of 'jammer' aircraft intent on suppressing enemy defences, top-cover fighters, more Tornado bombers, reconnaissance planes, AWACS early-warning, intelligence-gathering and target-identification aircraft, and the deadly, delta-winged F-117A Stealth fighter-bombers. The latter, invisible to enemy radar and often mistaken for UFOs, were likened by many to 'ghost' planes.

In no time at all, nocturnal Baghdad was illuminated by the greatest fireworks display in history and covered by an enormous umbrella of turbulent black smoke.

In the first 24 hours of this incredibly complex, computer-controlled war, over a thousand sorties were flown and over a hundred missiles launched against 158 targets, including communications centres and Scud launching sites, with as many as twelve combat aircraft being refuelled in-flight simultaneously by tankers stacked six deep in the air.

During the day, the first Allied casualty was the loss of a single Tornado. During the night of the seventeenth, however, from Iraqi airfields and secret bases in the west of the country, Saddam's military commanders unleashed a volley of eight Scud missiles at Israel. Two landed in Haifa and four in Tel Aviv. They were followed immediately by more Scud attacks on Riyadh, where the War Room and main communications of the Coalition effort were located.

Even as the citizens of Haifa, Tel Aviv and Riyadh were donning NBC suits, designed for use during nuclear, biological or chemical attack, or placing gas masks over their heads, Patriot anti-missile missiles were taking off with a deafening cacophony. These were followed rapidly by an equally loud din overhead as the incoming Scuds were hit and exploded, filling the sky with great flashes of silvery light, mushrooms of black smoke and spectacular webs of crimson tracers and downward-curving streams of dazzling white, yellow and blood-red flame.

By the second day of the war, RAF aircrews were attempting to trap Iraqi aircraft hidden in hardened aircraft shelters, or HASs, by bombing the access tracks and taxiways leading from the shelters to the runways. At the same time, US giant B52s were carrying out round-the-clock, high-altitude attritional bombing raids designed to demoralize, exhaust and daze the Iraqi troops by denying them sleep, when not actually killing them.

By Day Three, however, it had become clear that the major threat to the Coalition was the Scuds, particularly those on mobile launchers.

'Which is where we come in,' Major Hailsham told his assembled troopers outside his tent in the FOB in Al Jubail. 'The difficulty in tracking mobile Scud launchers is complicated by Saddam's use of dummy rockets that look realistic from the air and contain fuel that explodes when hit by a bomb, thereby encouraging our pilots to report more strikes than they've actually made. They also use dummy mobile launchers with real crews and they, too, look genuine from the air.'

'You mean the crews of the dummy mobile launchers have to drive around the desert, deliberately trying to be spotted, in order to misdirect the fire from our aircraft?'

'Correct,' Hailsham said.

'Some job!' Geordie exclaimed. 'Rather them than me! Driving around just to be picked off by any passing aircraft and become another statistic on their kill counts. No, thanks. Not *my* cup of tea!'

'As if those Air Force bastards don't already come out with enough bullshit when they're doing their sums,' Andrew said, flashing his perfect teeth. 'The day I find an honest Air Force kill count I'll eat my own cock.'

'*If* you can find it,' Geordie said, which brought the house down.

OK, men, that's enough,' Hailsham admonished them, continuing when he had regained their attention: 'It's becoming clear that because of these dummy sites and launchers, the number of Scuds taken out by the aircrews is considerably

43

less than at first anticipated. And as the real ones can't be seen from the air, eyeball recces and personal contact are needed. So, my good fellows, we're going to take them out ourselves, with particular emphasis on those within range of Israel, located in the desert round two Iraqi airfields known only as H2 and H3. So far, the Israelis are refusing to be drawn into the war. We therefore have to stop the Scud attacks on Israel before their patience wears out.'

'What's the terrain like around H2 and H3?' Ricketts asked.

'Fortunately a lot of it's less flat and open than most parts of the desert,' replied Hailsham, using his pointer to indicate the area on the map behind him. 'The demarcation line is between the British and US territories on the most distant of the three MSRs [military supply routes] running north-east from Baghdad to Amman. If the Americans operate mostly to the north of it, in the area they call Scud Boulevard, or the northern "Scud box", as they call it, and we keep to Scud Alley, south of the main road, there'll be no danger of us fighting each other accidentally. Our territory, Scud Alley, is the Jordanian lava plateau, a relatively high, hilly area with deep wadis that are often flash-flooded after storms. Loose rock instead of sand, though dense sandstorms are blown in from other areas. Lots of rain instead of burning sun. Freezing cold at night. In fact, it's more like the Falklands than it is like Oman, so you shouldn't find it too strange.'

'I remember the Falklands well,' Paddy said. 'Rain, hail and snow.'

'Right,' Jock concurred. 'OPs always flooded with water. Fucking wind every day. I thought this place would be a pleasant change – balmy nights, lots of sunshine.'

'You just want to look like me,' Andrew teased him. 'Suntanned and beautiful.'

'Spare me!' Jock retorted.

'That's enough,' said Hailsham, with a wave of his hand. 'Let's get back to the business in hand.'

'Yes, boss,' Geordie said, grinning mischievously at each of his mates in turn and cracking his knuckles.

'Good.' Glancing outside the lean-to tent, Hailsham saw the sun sinking towards the flat horizon, casting its crimson light on the white plain as darkness crept in. Helicopters and fighter planes were silhouetted in its huge, fiery eye like ink-black cut-outs suspended on invisible threads. From where he stood they looked beautiful. 'The Regiment will undertake three lines of attack,' he continued. 'Some teams will stake out static, covert road-watch patrols to report the movement of Scud traffic. Others will then vector F-15 strike aircraft onto the Scuds to destroy them.'

'What kind of teams?' asked Danny.

'Lurp teams – eight men. To be inserted by chopper at an LZ about 140 to 180 miles behind the enemy border, without any transport other than desert boots and a strong will.'

The 'Lurp' teams Hailsham referred to were LRRP, or long-range reconnaissance patrols.

'A strong will,' Andrew echoed with a devilish grin. 'That whittles it down to one man – me – and that isn't enough.'

'In parallel,' Hailsham said when the anticipated scorn had been poured on Andrew, 'there'll be fighting columns of up to a dozen well-armed Land Rovers carrying one and a half tons of war *matériel* each, manned by a half squadron of thirty men or more. We'll have four such columns. Their job will be to penetrate one of two major areas in the west, near the border with Jordan, from where the Scuds are launched. This "Scud box" is a well-defended area of desert of approximately 240 square miles, including the motorway linking Baghdad with Amman. Around twelve to fourteen mobile launchers are thought to be in or near the area.'

'Do we move by day or night?' Ricketts asked.

'It's not the Empty Quarter, so we'll mostly move by night. According to Intelligence, Bedouin come and go constantly. There's also a surprising amount of civilian traffic, much of it generated by fear of Western vengeance on Baghdad. Last but not least, because it's a critically important military zone, it's filled with Iraqi military personnel of all kinds, including Scud crews and the militia.'

'How do we insert?' said Andrew.

'Two of the OP patrols will go in on foot. Another will be lifted in by RAF Chinooks. The rest will drive in on stripped-down Land Rovers and motorbikes. We cross the border on the twentieth – tomorrow.'

'Who does what?' asked Danny.

'Allocation of duties is being drawn up right now and you'll all be informed within the hour. Any more questions?'

'No, boss,' was the general response.

'OK, men, go and have some chow. Get as much rest as possible. You'll get your allocations later. Departure time will be the afternoon or early evening. That's it. Class dismissed.' As the men turned away, heading for the mess tent, Hailsham indicated that Ricketts should remain. 'I have a special job for you,' he said. 'Pull up a chair, Sergeant-Major.'

Ricketts sat in a wooden chair on the other side of the trestle table Hailsham was using as a desk. The major placed two cups on the table and removed the cap from a vacuum flask. 'Tea?' he asked. When Ricketts nodded, he poured two cups of hot, white tea, then pushed one over to Ricketts. 'Sorry, Sergeant-Major, no sugar.' He glanced out over the sea of tents, now sinking back into a crimson twilight streaked with great shadows. After sipping some tea, he turned back to Ricketts. 'Before anyone goes anywhere,' he said, 'we have to cut Iraq's links with the outside world. They're in the shape of a complex web of communications towers known as microwave links, set up in the desert, danger- ously close to main roads and supply routes.'

'Should be easy to find,' Ricketts said, trying his hot tea.

'Not that easy, Sergeant-Major. The towers may be visible, but the fibre-optic cables are buried well below ground. So far, even the

US National Security Council's combined intelligence and scientific know-how hasn't been able to bug them or tap into them – let alone destroy them.'

Ricketts spread his hands in the air, indicating bewilderment. 'So how do we knock out Iraq's whole communications system? It's too widespread, boss.'

'We don't necessarily have to knock the whole system out,' Hailsham said. 'According to the green slime, it's the communications system coming out of Baghdad that controls Saddam's trigger-finger. Like the rest of the system, that network is a mixture of microwave link towers, in which telecom messages are transmitted short distances by air waves, and by fibre-optic cables buried in the ground and capable of carrying an enormous amount of data. We've received enough info from Intelligence to enable us to concentrate on the fibre-optic cables. Those lines carry Baghdad's orders to the Iraqi troops responsible for Scud operations. They also run Saddam Hussein's diplomatic traffic to Amman, Geneva, Paris and the UN, thus increasing his political credibility. It's our job to destroy that credibility as well as the Scuds – and we have to do it immediately.'

'You mean tonight?'

'Exactly. I want you to pick 40 of your most reliable men and have them ready to be airlifted before midnight. I'm coming with you. Our LZ is an area approximately sixty kilometres south of Baghdad, near the main road that leads to Basra. According to Intelligence, the highest density of Baghdad's fibre-optic cables are buried there and the ground is relatively easy to dig. We're going to dig down, remove a sample of cable for analysis, then blow up the rest – so we need a couple of demolition experts. Any questions, Ricketts?'

'No questions, boss.'

'I'm delighted to hear it. Have you finished your tea?'

'Yes.'

'Then go to it.'

Ricketts grinned, finished his tea, then stood up and left the tent. Heading back to his own lean-to, he was enthralled by the sight of so many tents on the dark plain, under the desert's starlit sky, but even more thrilled – indeed almost ecstatic – to be back in business at last.

It was what he and most of his mates lived for.

4

At approximately midnight, two of the RAF's CH-47 twin-blade Chinooks lifted Ricketts's chosen team of 40 men off the airstrip of the FOB and headed through the night sky for the LZ. The men, packed into the gloomy, noisy interior of the helicopter, were wearing the normal beige beret, but without its winged-dagger badge and now camouflaged under a *shemagh*, or veil, that could also be wrapped around the eyes and mouth to protect them from dust and sand. (The same kind of veil was used to camouflage the standard 7.62mm SLR, or self-loading rifle.) The standard-issue woollen pullover was woven in colours that would blend in with the desert floor and matched the colouring of the high-topped, lace-up desert boots.

'I feel like an A-rab,' Geordie said. 'What do I look like?'

'Real cute,' Paddy replied.

'I always knew you adored me.'

Most of the men were armed either with the ubiquitous semi-automatic SLR or with 30-round, semi- and fully automatic M16s and their many attachments, including bayonets, bipods for accuracy when firing from the prone position, telescopic sights, night-vision aids, and M203 40mm grenade-launchers. Some had Heckler & Koch MP5 30-round sub-machine-guns. A few had belt-fed L7A2 7.62mm general-purpose machine-guns, or GPMGs, capable of firing 800 rounds a minute to a range of up to 1400 metres. All had standard-issue Browning FN 9mm high-power handguns on their hips, capable of firing 13 rounds in a couple of seconds.

These weapons and their bulky ammunition belts, combined with the standard bergens and camouflaging, made the men look awkward and bulky, almost Neanderthal. However, those weapons were only part of their personal equipment, and other, heavier weapons were taking up what little space they had left between them.

In case they were approached by tanks during the operation, the men were also carrying heavy support weapons, including the 94mm light anti-tank weapon, or LAW 80, which fired a high-explosive anti-tank (HEAT) rocket and could be used on bunkers as well as armoured vehicles; the portable FIM-92A Stinger anti-aircraft missile system, capable of firing a heat-seeking missile 8000 metres and fitted with a friend or foe identification, or FFI, system; and two different mortars: the 51mm mortar, which, though carried and operated by one man, could launch an HE bomb to a range of 750 metres, and the larger, heavier 81mm mortar, which required three men to carry it, but could fire HE bombs 5660 metres at a rate of eight rounds per minute.

'Tell me, Alfie,' Andrew said, bored out of his mind, and deciding to have a bit of sport with Sergeant Alfred Lloyd, who was sitting beside him, 'how come you're almost as tall as me, but only half of my weight?'

'I'm taller than you, fella, by half an inch. I can tell when our eyes meet.'

A dour Leicester man and SAS demolition specialist who had formerly been a Royal Engineer, then an ammunition technician with the Royal Army Ordnance Corps, Lloyd had unkempt red hair, a beakish, broken nose, and a lean face veined by booze and scorched by the sun.

'I'm always willing to give a man the benefit

of the doubt,' Andrew said, 'so how come, since you're even *taller* than me, you only weigh half my size?'

'I've sabotaged ships, aircraft, every type of armoured vehicle, power stations, communications centres, supply depots, railways and roads. It required a lot of climbing and running, which is why I'm still slim.'

Alfie Lloyd was indeed still as thin as a rake, though now heavily burdened like the others and divided from big Andrew by the boxes packed with explosives, charges, detonator caps and the many other tools of his dangerous trade. Andrew stared at them sceptically.

'Those bloody explosives, man, are they safe?'

'Sure.'

'I've heard that explosives go off real easy.'

'Bullshit. Most explosives are safe unless they're deliberately set off. You can hammer TNT into powdered crystals and it still won't explode. That's why it can be delivered by parachute. No problem at all.'

'Mmmmm,' Andrew murmured, not totally convinced. 'So what exactly *is* explosive, man? Give it to me in simple words.'

Alfie thought for a while, wondering how to reply, not being a man of great eloquence and aware that Andrew was a poet, slick with his tongue. Finally he said, 'You tell me.'

Andrew nodded and beamed.

'A solid or liquid substance which, under the influence of a certain stimulus, such as an exploding detonator, is rapidly converted into another substance with accompanying high pressure, leading to the outburst of violence and noise known as an explosion. What say you, Sergeant?'

'Is that fucking Swahili?'

'I'm from Barbados,' Andrew replied, 'where they only speak English.'

'You could have fooled me,' Alfie said, shaking his head. 'I thought *I* spoke English!'

'They only *think* they speak English in Barbados,' Paddy Clarke said. 'All that molasses and rum goes to their heads and makes them think they're white men. We should hand Andrew over to a missionary for a little correction.'

'The Paddy from Liverpool has spoken,' Andrew intoned. 'Let us bow down and throw up.'

'Can it, the lot of you,' the RAF Loadmaster barked at them as he materialized from the gloom. He glanced through one of the portholes in the passenger hold and announced: 'We're coming in, if we're lucky, to the LZ, so prepare to offload.'

'Yes, mother!' Taff chimed in a high, school-boy's voice, though he quickly made a great show of checking his gear when the Loadmaster gave him a baleful stare.

'Hey, Moorcock' Paddy said, turning to the new man beside him, eager for a little sport. 'Where did you say you were located before you were badged?'

'The Welsh Guards,' Moorcock answered, giving his kit a great deal of attention.

'See any action?' Paddy asked him.

'A brief tour of Northern Ireland,' Moorcock said, sliding his arms awkwardly through the webbing of his bergen. 'Though I didn't see much there.'

'Know much about the Iraqis?'

'No.'

'They're fuckin' murderous bastards. Don't on any account let yourself be caught. There's things worse than death, kid.'

'What's that, Corporal?' Trooper Stone asked with a grin, being less impressionable than his friend. Although he, like Moorcock and Gillett, had only recently been badged and was serving his probationary period, he wasn't about to take any bullshit from the older hands. 'What's worse than death, then?'

'They'll pull your nails out,' Paddy said.

'They'll gang-bang you,' Jock added.

'They'll chop your cock off and make you eat it with couscous,' Geordie put in. 'Then they'll cut your eyeballs out and make you suck them until you go gaga.'

'Go fuck yourselves,' Trooper Stone said.

'Leave these poor probationers alone,' threatened Andrew, 'or I'll personally chop *your* cocks off and shove them, all shrivelled, up your arses, which will then need some wiping.'

'Thanks, Sergeant,' Trooper Moorcock said, tightening the straps on his bergen and looking serious while his two friends, Stone and Gillett, grinned at each other.

'We're touching down,' the Loadmaster said. 'Hold on to your balls, lads . . . Three, two, one, zero . . . *Touchdown!*'

The transport landed with a lot of bouncing, roaring and metallic shrieking, but otherwise no problems, on an LZ located about half a mile from the main road that ran one way to Basra, 40 miles the other way to Baghdad.

The men disembarked even before the two Chinooks' engines had gone into neutral, spilling out of the side into dense clouds of sand whipped up by the twin-bladed rotors. When the billowing sand had subsided, the first thing they saw was a fantastic display of fireworks illuminating the distant horizon: immense webs of red and purple anti-aircraft fire, silvery-white explosions, showers of crimson sparks and streams of phosphorus fireflies.

'Baghdad,' Hailsham explained to those nearest to him. 'The Allies are bombing the hell out of it. Rather them than us.'

As their eyes adjusted to moonlit darkness, they saw the nearest two microwave links, soaring high above the flat plain, about a quarter mile apart, but less than twenty yards from the road. Spreading out and keeping their weapons at the ready, the men hiked across the dusty, wind-blown plain until they reached a point equidistant between the two towers. From here, the road was dangerously close – a mere twenty-odd yards.

'It's pretty dark,' Ricketts said, glancing in every direction, 'so if anyone comes along the road, we should be OK if we stay low. We need sentries on point in both directions, with the men not being used for digging keeping guard in LUPs.'

'Right,' Hailsham said.

Ricketts gave his instructions by means of hand signals. With the Chinooks waiting on the ground a quarter of a mile away, their rotors turning quietly in neutral, the bulk of the men broke into four-man teams, then fanned out to form a circle of LUPs, or lying-up positions, from where they could keep their eyes on the road and defend the diggers and demolition team if anyone came along.

Meanwhile Hailsham and Ricketts accompanied Sergeant Lloyd as he checked the alignment between the two communications towers and gauged where the fibre-optic cable was running between them, hidden under the ground.

'This is it,' he said, waving his hand from left to right to indicate an invisible line between the two towers. He turned to the dozen troopers selected to dig. 'I want a series of four holes about twelve foot apart, each six foot long and as deep as you need to go to expose the cable. That should be about four feet. If you see any transport coming along that road, or if we call a warning to you, drop down into the hole you're digging and don't make a move until given clearance. OK, get going.'

The men laid down their weapons, removed

spades and shovels from their bergens, and proceeded to dig the holes as required. As they did so, they and the others – now stretched belly-down in LUPs on the dark ground, their weapons at the ready and covering the road in both directions – were able to watch the fantastic pyrotechnics of crimson anti-aircraft tracer fire and silvery bomb bursts over distant Baghdad, which was being bombed by wave after wave of British, American and Saudi jets, as well as Tomahawk Cruise missiles fired from ships in the Gulf, flying in at just under the speed of sound at heights of 50–250 feet, to cause more devastation and death.

'Wow!' Andrew whispered, looking at the lights over the distant city. 'That's just beautiful, man!'

'Beautiful from here,' Hailsham replied. 'Hell on earth if you're there.'

'You men,' Sergeant Lloyd said to two of his eight sappers, both of whom had various explosives, charges and timers dangling from their webbing. 'I want you to take out those towers, one to each man. Fix enough explosives to the base to make sure the whole caboodle topples over. Use electronic timers that can be fired from here by remote control. Don't make any mistakes. When this lot goes up, those towers have to go up at the same time. Understood?'

'Yes, boss,' the men nodded.

Then they headed off in opposite directions, towards the tower each had selected, the explosives on their webbing bouncing up and down as they ran.

'You see that?' Geordie whispered to Trooper Gillett, having decided to pass the time by winding him up. 'Those explosives are liable to go off any second, taking us out with him.'

'Aw, come off it, Geordie!'

'No, kid, it's true! I'd be pissing in my pants if I was you. He'll blow up any minute now.'

'That's bullshit, Geordie,' Trooper Stone retorted. 'We all heard what Sergeant Lloyd said in the plane – explosives don't blow up easily.'

'Besides,' Trooper Gillett added, 'that sapper's practically out of sight already. If the stupid bastard blows himself up, we're well out of range. Pull the other one, Geordie.'

'Shut up, you men,' Sergeant Lloyd said, glancing down at the men digging the holes, 'these men have to concentrate. If you've got nothing better to do, I can always hand you a shovel.'

'No, thanks,' Geordie said, edging away. 'I

have to go and stand out on point. Have a nice day!'

'Fucking nerd,' Sergeant Lloyd said.

The digging alone took forty-five minutes. During that time two vehicles, about half an hour apart, came along the road, heading away from Baghdad, their headlights cutting a swathe through the darkness but not picking out the men who were concealed in LUPs, guns at the ready, only twenty yards or so away. The first vehicle was a Mercedes saloon filled with white-robed Arabs; the second was a soft-topped army truck packed with Iraqi soldiers. Both passed by and disappeared into the night, their drivers and passengers, probably fleeing from the air attacks on Baghdad, not knowing how close to death they had come in what they thought was an empty, safe area.

About twenty minutes after the army truck had passed by, one of the men uncovered a fibre-optic cable.

'That's it,' Sergeant Lloyd said, glancing down into the hole as the trooper who had reached the first cable wiped sweat from his brow. 'I want that whole stretch of cable cleared, Trooper, so get back to your digging.'

'Right, Sarge,' the trooper said. He continued

his digging. When the length of cable running across the bottom of the hole was completely exposed, he jumped out to let Lloyd jump in. Ricketts glanced left and right, checking the road in both directions, but there was no sign of any more movement. Satisfied, he knelt beside the hole in which Lloyd, unpacking his boxes, was already at work.

'Cable!' a trooper called from the next hole.

'Me, too!' someone else called, to be followed by a third, then a fourth.

'Tell them to clear the whole length of cable,' Lloyd told Ricketts, 'then get out of the holes. My men will do the rest.'

'Right,' Ricketts said, then stood and went from hole to hole, passing on Lloyd's orders.

'I've reached mine,' a man in the fifth hole told him. 'There it is,' said a man in the sixth hole, looking down and pointing.

By the time Ricketts had passed on Lloyd's instructions, the first men had completely uncovered their cables and were clambering gratefully out of the holes to wipe the mud off their hands and have a drink of hot tea from a vacuum flask. As they did so, Lloyd's assistants, all former sappers, jumped down into the holes to fix explosive charges to the cables.

Major Hailsham was kneeling on the rim of Lloyd's hole, looking down as Lloyd worked, so Ricketts, just as interested, knelt beside him.

Even as Iraqi MiGs and Mirage F-1s flew overhead, heading away from the battered airfields of a spectacularly illuminated Baghdad, Sergeant Lloyd and his men coolly continued what they were doing. With Hailsham and Ricketts looking on, Lloyd sliced through a cable and slipped a piece into his bergen, to be shipped back to England for examination. He then packed C3/C4 plastic explosive around and between the exposed cables, fixed it in place, and attached a non-electrical firing system with a time fuse connected to a blasting cap in a thin aluminium tube, which he embedded carefully in the explosive charge. To the blasting cap he attached a detonating cord of reinforced primacord – a small, high-explosive core protected by half a dozen layers of material – which in turn was taped together with two primers and a detonator fixed to a timing device. He glanced up at Hailsham.

'Give us twenty minutes to get back to the choppers,' Hailsham said. 'That's all we need.'

'The other five started after me,' Lloyd replied, 'so I'll add on ten minutes.'

'Right,' Hailsham said, then turned to Ricketts as Lloyd set his timer. 'Signal the men to break up the LUPs and head back to the choppers.'

'Right, boss.' Ricketts used hand signals to convey Hailsham's instructions. From where he was standing, he saw nothing but dark emptiness, but then the men started appearing, rising up from the flat earth, silhouetted either by stars or the fireworks display over distant Baghdad. After strapping their bergens to their shoulders and picking up their weapons, they lumbered like misshapen beasts back towards the Chinooks, whose rotors were still spinning, though silently, their engines in neutral.

As the men retreated from the area, being swallowed up in darkness, Lloyd and his other demolition specialists emerged one by one from their separate holes, wiping the mud from their hands. While they were packing up their equipment, the other sappers returned and reported that they had placed the explosives and remote-control timing devices on the soaring communications towers. Satisfied, Sergeant Lloyd nodded, then led them all across the windswept plain, hurrying after the others.

Hailsham and Ricketts brought up the rear, the latter keeping his eye on the road. He saw nothing and finally turned away, walking faster to catch up with his men. When they reached the Chinooks, hazy behind the dust clouds swirling under the rotors, they gathered together to look back at the stretch of earth between the two towers. When Ricketts saw Hailsham and Lloyd checking their watches, he did the same. The whole job had taken ninety minutes so far.

Ricketts felt the ground shaking beneath his feet, then saw a dark eruption far ahead, equidistant between the silhouetted towers, where the holes had been dug in the ground. As the vibrations turned into a rumbling, the earth erupted in a dark crescent and then a black, expanding hillock. Then the rumbling became a thunderous explosion that created a gigantic mushroom cloud of smoke, dust, sand and showering gravel, billowing up from a bed of white and blue flames fringed by crimson sparks. The mushroom cloud rose higher, expanded in all directions and was blotting out the stars even as its tendrils coiled languorously back down to shower the desert floor with its deadly debris. As one tower, then the other, collapsed and disappeared in the billowing smoke, the roaring tapered off into a rumbling and eventually faded into silence.

'Let's go!' Hailsham bawled.

Reluctantly, the men turned their backs on the spectacle before them, filed back into the Chinooks and were lifted off the desert plain before Iraqi troops arrived at the scene of the explosion, which they surely would.

When his Chinook had ascended and was heading back to Saudi Arabia, Ricketts glanced back through a porthole and saw the immense mushroom cloud settling down over what looked like an enormous crater surrounded by charred, upturned earth. Where the two towers had stood, there was now just a mess of tangled metal, spreading out a great distance.

With communications from Baghdad cut, the real fight could start.

5

The men chosen for long-range reconnaissance patrols, or 'Lurps', were given light-strike vehicles, or LSVs, and Land Rover 90s, more commonly known in SAS circles as 'Pink Panthers' or 'dinkies'. Each Pink Panther was a mobile arsenal, carrying a Magellan satellite navigation system, two M203 grenade-launchers, LAW 80 94mm anti-tank missiles, a front-mounted 7.62-mm GPMG, a rear-mounted 0.5in Browning heavy machine-gun, as well as Stinger anti-aircraft missiles for use against Iraqi helicopter gunships. The commander and driver were each given a pair of Litton night-vision goggles. An armed trooper from the Mobility Group was to accompany each Pink Panther on a motorbike. Each team also carried a laser designator to be used for marking targets for the Allied aircraft, whose laser-guided bombs could then home in accurately on air-defence sites, bunkers, radar sites, command-and-control centres and military factories.

At approximately midnight on 22 January two RAF Chinooks lifted a squadron of SAS men and their LSVs and Pink Panthers deep into the desert of western Iraq, in the area known as Scud Alley.

Looking through a porthole just before landing, Ricketts saw some of the US HH-531J Pave Low and HH-60G Night Hawk helicopters just below and ahead. Equipped with special electronic and night-flying systems, they were extremely efficient as pathfinders. They were, however, also transporting Pink Panthers, LSVs and Honda motorbikes, all of which were slung in nets below them and seemed to be flying just above the desert plain. The others, which Ricketts could not see, were slung below the Chinooks.

Turning away from the porthole and glancing around the helicopter's long, narrow, dark hold, Ricketts saw the men preparing for the landing. Coming on this insertion straight after the previous night's raid on the communications towers near Baghdad, Ricketts and most of the men were particularly tired. And yet they were glad to be back in business, instead of wasting their time in so-called further training on the hot, dusty plains of the Empty Quarter.

With the appearance of their RAF Loadmaster, Ricketts knew they were about to land. This was confirmed when the Chinook slowed down, stopping moving forward, hovered briefly, then made its vertical descent. When the Loadmaster shouted over the din for the men to prepare to unload, they all checked their safety belts, equipment and weapons while firing off the usual bullshit.

The Chinook hovered for some time while its underslung loads – the Land Rovers, LSVs and motorbikes – were set down gently and released, but eventually it moved forward, away from the disengaged loads, and touched down on the desert floor further on. It bounced lightly a few times, then its roar subsided as its rotors, though still spinning, went into neutral. The loading ramp was opened, allowing moonlight to beam in as the men disembarked.

Once outside, Ricketts was shocked by the cold, fierce wind. Tying his *shemagh* across his face to protect his nose and mouth from the swirling sand, he noticed the other men were doing the same. With their veils and the camouflaging over their berets, they looked like Arab militiamen.

The sky was clear of clouds, but the sweeping sand obscured the stars and the horizon was barely visible through the murk. The dropped vehicles, still in their netting, were about a hundred yards further back and the other two Chinooks, each of which held 44 fully equipped troops, were about to land about the same distance away in the opposite direction.

The first helicopter touched down without trouble. When the second followed, luckily a good distance away, the ground erupted beneath it with a mighty roar, spewing soil, sand and smoke. The wheels in contact with the ground were blown off by the blast, burst into flames and shot like rapidly spinning balls of fire through the billowing black smoke. The Chinook crashed down on its rear end, then tilted sideways, its rotors still spinning, barely missing the ground. Where the wheels had been, the fuselage was torn open and the twisted metal was scorched.

'Damn!' Major Hailsham explained. 'They've landed on a minefield!' He started forward instinctively, without thinking, but Ricketts grabbed his elbow and pulled him back. 'You're right, boss – it's a bloody minefield. There's not a thing we can do.' Understanding what Ricketts meant,

Hailsham nodded, then looked back across the dark plain.

The Chinook was not on fire, but its underside was badly damaged and the fuselage was shuddering violently as the pilot, knowing the men could not disembark, tried to lift off. As the troopers pouring out of the other Chinook milled about, looking at the damaged chopper and then glancing cautiously at the ground near their feet, wondering if they too were on a minefield, the damaged, tilting Chinook roared and shook even more, its rotors spinning faster, creating great clouds of sand. Slowly, with metallic shrieks of protest, it righted itself and lifted off the ground.

As the Chinook rose awkwardly and noisily from the minefield, obscured in its own swirling curtains of sand, dust and debris, Jock McGregor, in charge of a crackling PRC 319 portable radio system, called out to Captain Hailsham: 'The captain says to tell you he can't land without wheels, so he wants permission to return to the FOB and take his chances on a landing there.'

'Permission granted!' Hailsham bellowed against the combined noise of the roaring Chinook and the howling wind. 'Wish him good luck.'

'Aye, aye, boss!' Jock called back, waving

his hand in acknowledgement. He conveyed Hailsham's message over the radio as the Chinook reached flight altitude, hovered for a moment, then laboriously headed back towards Saudi Arabia, leaving an immense cloud of sand to settle over the minefield.

Hailsham's hazel eyes turned above his fluttering light-brown *shemagh* to look directly at Ricketts. 'Damn!' he exclaimed softly. 'Forty-four men down already. Ah, well, let's get started.'

The rest of the men from Hailsham's Chinook had already surrounded the vehicles and equipment disengaged from the underslung loads and were removing the nets in which they had been carried. Hailsham and Ricketts joined them. Glancing across the desert, they saw that the men from the second Chinook were doing the same. Hailsham called Jock over and asked for the microphone for his PRC 319, which he used for a chat with the NCO commanding the other group. Satisfied that they were all right, he told them to keep their eyes peeled for any sign of land-mines elsewhere.

'The first thing we have to do,' he said to Ricketts, handing the mike back to Jock, 'is get rid of that damned minefield over there.'

He waited until the conveyance netting had been removed from the first Pink Panther and the satellite communications system fixed to the vehicle, then called HQ in Riyadh, giving his grid reference and asking for an AWACS command aircraft to fly over and detonate the whole minefield. Receiving an affirmative, he turned off the SATCOM system and watched his men as they removed the netting from the other vehicles, attached the separately packed equipment, and prepared the vehicles for use.

The Pink Panthers were painted in a desert camouflage scheme of sunset pink, earth brown and sandy yellow, which made them look a bit like cartoon or funfair cars. They were, however, highly sophisticated vehicles, with 3.5-litre V-8 petrol engines, five-speed gearboxes, alternating four- or five-wheel drive, with cabins stripped down to the hull and windscreens removed. They were also bristling with machine-guns and heavily laden with bergens, ammunition bandoliers, camping equipment and radios. Short-burst radio and SATCOM antennae were fixed to the sides, jutting up in the air, high above the multidirectional barrels of the guns. A SATNAV Global Positioning System (GPS) receiver was mounted on the vehicle – though it could also be carried by hand – and a sun compass, also used for navigation, was mounted horizontally on the front. Smoke dischargers were fitted front and rear, detachable searchlights were positioned on each side, camouflage netting was rolled across the bonnet and there were extra storage racks for food, water, fuel, spare parts, more weapons, ammunition and the tools required for the construction of OPs, or observation posts.

The LSVs, based on the dune-buggies widely used on American beaches, were virtually no more than tubular-steel frames in roll cages – no roof, body panels or windscreen – with two seats in the middle, fat, low-pressure tyres on each corner and a powerful engine. But although their payload capacity was limited, they carried LAW 80 anti-tank rockets and man-portable MILAN guided-missile firing posts, which made them ideal for hit-and-run raids on enemy targets.

The motorbikes, one to accompany each Land Rover, were Honda production machines, used as outriders, mainly for forward-observation purposes in terrain impassable to the other vehicles. They were driven mostly by daring young cowboys armed with an M16 slung across the back and a Browning 9mm high-power handgun in a holster at the hip.

A sudden, staccato series of mechanical coughs and roaring reminded Hailsham and Ricketts of the troopers disgorged from the second Chinook. Looking sideways, they saw that they were starting up their Pink Panthers, LSVs and motorbikes even as the Chinook was lifting off in a swirling cloud of sand and gravel. That cloud swallowed the men below, but they soon burst out of it, driving their assorted, brightly coloured vehicles across the flat plain to encircle Hailsham's group and skid to a halt, churning up more sand and dust. Meanwhile the Chinook behind Hailsham and Ricketts also took off, soon joining the other in the sky, where they hovered close together for a moment, like giant copulating beetles, before heading back to the border.

When the men around Hailsham had settled down, he climbed up on the back of his chosen Land Rover and called them in around him for his final briefing.

'First,' he said, 'I want to remind you that following Iraq's launch of Scud missiles against Israel, destroying their mobile launchers has become our number one priority. We're here because conventional aerial reconnaissance methods are too slow to keep track of the highly mobile missiles, so improvised methods have to be adapted to put the Scuds out of business. This area is a Scud box known as Scud Alley. It's about 240 square miles – including the motorway linking Baghdad with Amman. For that reason, it's very well defended and we have to be on our toes.'

'Does that mean we only move by night?' Danny Porter asked.

'This is no Empty Quarter. In short, it's damned dangerous. So, yes, we move only by night.'

Andrew had been studying his map and now he looked up. 'How many mobile launchers in this particular area?'

'Around twelve to fourteen – and we're going to find them.'

'What happens when we do?'

'The USAF and US Navy have put heavily armed F-15Es, F-16 Fighting Falcons, A-10s and A-6E Intruders on round-the-clock patrols over the Scud boxes, both north, where their men are, and south, where we are. However, the pilots need precise targeting information before they can launch attacks. We've been sent in here as mobile teams to put eyes on the ground. For this purpose we'll set up covert OPs to cover key roads. When Scud convoys are spotted, we'll either mark the target with our laser designators or pass the grid reference on to an E-3 AWACS command aircraft, using our SATCOM systems.'

'We just roam freely?' Geordie asked.

'Strictly within the area marked for your own team on the maps. Two Land Rovers, one LSV and one Honda to each patrol. We break up right now. We keep in touch with each other with short-burst transmissions on the PRC 319s. We rendezvous for resupplies at midnight five days from now – in Wadi Tubal, also marked on your maps. If anyone has any problems getting back, he's to contact the others by radio. Any questions?'

'Yeah,' Paddy Clarke said, putting up his hand like a schoolboy. 'What the hell are we doing with American LSVs instead of just the Pink Panthers? The fucking things only have a range of 200 kilometres against a dinkie's 650. Bloody useless, boss, if you ask me.'

'It's a trial run,' Hailsham explained. 'The LSVs are particularly popular with the US Special Forces, including those operating in the northern Scud box. I agree that they're small and have a much shorter range, but they're also extremely powerful and can go where the Land Rovers can't. Also, their relatively quiet engines and reduced radar and infrared signatures make them pretty difficult to find or hit. The American Delta Force strongly recommends them, so we're trying them out, with particular regard to their speed and mobility over difficult terrain. Any *more* questions?' When their shaking heads told him no, he said, 'Right, men, let's hit the road.'

After the Troop had been divided up into individual teams, the men climbed into their allocated vehicles and prepared to take off. Ricketts was commander of one of the Pink Panthers, sitting up front beside the driver, Danny Porter, with Geordie in the rear compartment as gunner, in charge of the 360-degree-traverse Browning 0.5in-calibre machine-gun. Andrew and Paddy were in the accompanying LSV and a young trooper, John 'Johnny Boy' Willoughby was on the Honda outrider, with his *shemagh* over his mouth and eyes, his M16 across his shoulders and his Browning at his hip.

With their veils, night-vision goggles and exposed facial skin camouflaged in blackening 'cam' cream, the men looked like brigands from a 'Mad Max' film.

Hailsham was just about to give the signal to move out when Jock, handling the SATCOM system in his Pink Panther, told him an RAF

Tornado was on its way to detonate the mine-field. In less than a minute they heard it overhead and Hailsham confirmed the grid readings to the pilot over the SATCOM.

'With all due respect, sir,' the pilot responded, his voice distorted by static, 'I think you should get the hell out of there before I drop my impressive load. You're a mite too close for comfort.'

'Thank you, Captain,' Hailsham replied, deadpan. 'I think I know what you mean. We'll be gone by the time you get here. Over and out.' Immediately, he gave the signal to move out, which was conveyed by his NCOs from one vehicle to another. Suddenly the desert's silence was split by the roaring of the Land Rovers, the lesser clamour of the LSVs and the harsh chatter of the motorbikes as they revved up. Hailsham's Pink Panther left first, heading deeper into the desert, and as the other vehicles followed him, one after the other, they churned up an enormous cloud of sand and dust.

This was nothing compared to the cloud created by the exploding JP233 bombs of the Tornado when it swooped down five minutes later. By that time the SAS mobile patrols had gathered much further out on the plain, waiting to see the results of the air attack.

Even in the moonlight, the Tornado was an awesome vision, a beast of many limbs and appendages, beginning with its air-to-air refuelling probe and including massive, moveable 'swing' wings; a high fin with ESM, or electronic surveillance measure; underslung fuel tanks and alarm anti-radar missiles; plus underwing ECM, or electronic countermeasure, pods, and protruding TRB 199 twin engines. For all that, it was a monster of terrible beauty, gifted with terrain-following radar and a computerized cockpit that enabled it to fly in as low as fifty feet above the ground to drop its JP233 bombs.

The bombs, which included a series of cratering devices, drifted down from the aircraft by parachute and detonated just above the ground. That detonation propelled various charges deep into the ground, and when these exploded they heaved up the surface and created many large holes beneath it. The multiple, underground explosions caused a vast area of the desert floor to rumble and shake. Then it erupted in a spectacular, cataclysmic mushroom cloud of sand, dust, gravel, smoke and swirling tendrils of gaseous flame. The noise was deafening, the impact shattering, and the mushroom expanded to form a great canopy over the desert, blotting out the big moon and brilliant stars.

Only when the great mushroom cloud had started to collapse, falling back in upon itself, did the men in the Land Rovers, LSVs and motorbikes head off in the opposite direction, away from Saudi Arabia and deeper into Iraq, eventually going off in many different directions, cutting lines through the desert.

They were all on their own now.

6

The Scuds, genuine and false, had been reported
as travelling along roads and tracks known as
MSRs, or military supply routes. The SAS patrols
had therefore each been given a preselected
stretch of MSR to cover. Driving by night for
an hour or so through the desert, with the
Pink Panther and the LSV side by side, and
the motorbike in the lead, Ricketts's group soon
reached the area selected for their OP, located
behind a ridge that offered a good view of the
MSR below.

As they would be here for five days, they dug
a large, deep, rectangular OP with one narrow
end as the rest bay, the other, facing the MSR,
for the observers and sentry, and a kit-well
in the middle, holding weapons, ammunition,
radio equipment, spare batteries, water cans
and dry food. The OP was covered in canvas,

SOLDIER A: SAS

which in turn was camouflaged with sand and gravel taken from the surrounding area, and the observation bay was screened by black hessian and contained a black-painted telescope on a tripod, as well as binoculars, night-vision aids, a camera, spare film, aerial photos previously taken by reconnaissance planes, codes and ciphers for radio transmissions, and logbooks and maps.

The weather in that area was exceptionally harsh, much colder than expected, and before the night was over they found themselves working in a dense cloud of freezing fog. By the time a blood-red sun rose over the flat horizon, bringing with it the heat, they all realized that they were in for extremes of hot and cold, with the accompanying threat of sunstroke or dehydration in the daylight, and hypothermia in the damp, freezing night.

Nevertheless the OP was completed just before full daylight came, with the spoil removed and scattered over the ground a good distance away. The vehicles were then covered in camouflage nets with hessian stitched in to keep out the sunlight.

Though they all had water bottles, the men knew the water would not last long, so while Danny and Geordie kept watch for enemy activity and the others sorted out the equipment in the OP, Jock expertly constructed a desert still.

After choosing the nearby spot where water would be most likely to collect, Jock dug a hole one metre deep and two metres wide, then filled it with vegetation soaked in his own urine. He placed a metal container in the centre, covered it with plastic sheeting with a rough undersurface, cut a hole in it and slid a drinking tube through the hole, leaving one end inside the container, the other extending out to the side. The sheeting was held down by stones placed around its circumference, with another couple of stones in the centre to depress the covering directly over the container. This simple device would provide up to a litre of drinking water every twenty-four hours by collecting the condensation that would form beneath the plastic and drip into the container.

'I'm not sure I can drink this,' Geordie said, 'knowing that the condensation was caused by your piss.'

'Right,' Paddy agreed. 'When we think of where that dick of yours has been, we want to know what your piss is like. These days a man can get AIDS just by breathing the air, so I think the water made from your condensation could be as deadly as cyanide.'

'You don't want to drink my water,' Jock replied, 'then *don't* drink my water. Who's inviting you, anyway?'

As for their own waste, the men excreted or urinated well away from the OP and either buried it or, in the latter case, let the ground soak it up.

'Personally,' Geordie said, 'I'm used to having a bog indoors, but Sergeant Winston, whose ancestors were not like yours and mine, probably thinks the cool breeze on his bare arse is a natural laxative.'

'At least it comes out of my arse,' Andrew replied without a pause, 'whereas with you, being a miraculous being, it comes out the top end.'

'Complete with lots of hot air,' Paddy added. 'Known as farting and wind.'

'In Newcastle they think that's civilized conversation,' 'Johnny Boy' Willoughby butted in, getting the measure of the company he was keeping and revelling in it. 'But up there they would, wouldn't they?'

'Amen to that,' Andrew said.

When everything was completed and they had settled down to their surveillance – some on guard, some on watch, Hailsham and Ricketts planning their raids on the likely Scud bunkers marked on their maps – Hailsham decided to send the half-crazy young Johnny Boy off on his Honda for eyeball reconnaissance of certain areas.

'You will also report on the movements of any military traffic across the desert or along the MSRs,' Hailsham said. 'Do you think you can do that, Trooper?'

'Yes, boss!' Johnny Boy snapped. Blond-haired, blue-eyed and handsome, he had nerves of steel and was as good as Niki Lauda on his motorbike, though more reckless. 'Scud bunkers, mobile units and any other military traffic on the desert or along the MSRs – you want it, you've got it, boss.'

'No derring-do,' Ricketts warned him. 'No personally favoured adventures. You stay out of sight where it's possible to do so, and you don't fire a shot unless fired upon. Is that understood?'

'Yes, boss! Absolutely!'

'We've heard stories about you, Trooper.'

'Fame at last, boss! What stories?'

'Reckless behaviour,' Hailsham told him. 'Courting danger for the hell of it. An irresistible impulse to be seen by the enemy and try to play cat-and-mouse with them. Any truth in it, Trooper?'

'Bloody scandalous, boss. Careless tongues and idle gossip. Since I'm usually out there on my own, how would anyone know that? No, boss, I'm A1 on this.'

'You have the benefit of the doubt,' Ricketts said, 'so don't let us down, Trooper. On your way and good luck.'

'Aye, aye, boss,' Johnny Boy said.

He left wearing his camouflaged SAS beret without the winged-dagger badge, his *shemagh* to cover his mouth and nose, and tinted spectacles to protect his eyes. An M16 rifle was slung across his back, a Browning 9mm high-power handgun sat on his hip, a leather-cased Fairburn-Sykes commando knife had been slipped down the inside of one of his desert boots, and he had carrier bags on either side of his motorbike. Taking off in a cloud of sand, he soon became a mere cloud in the distance and eventually disappeared.

As the desert was vast and relatively feature-less, Johnny Boy would navigate generally with the sun compass mounted horizontally on the handlebars of his motorbike. For more precise positioning, particularly when calling in enemy positions to the OP, he would rely on the portable GPS receiver he had brought along in one of the carrier bags. By comparing coded signals from various satellites in fixed orbits around the earth, the GPS could calculate its position to within fifteen metres, but its complex electronics could fail, which is why the less accurate, though more reliable sun compass was always carried as well.

Using short-burst transmissions on the PRC 319, Ricketts was able to keep in touch with the other patrols, first learning that they were all OK and in their OP positions, then gradually building up a coherent picture of what they were doing and finding. Some had broken the rule of not travelling during the day and already taken out Scud bunkers and mobile launchers, either by calling down air strikes or, in the case of mobile launchers, doing it themselves before the launchers moved on.

'It was too damned frustrating,' Hailsham informed Ricketts by radio, 'to see the mobile launchers passing by untouched or the bunkers right in front of us, undefended. Time's too short for considerations of safety. We've got to take them all out.'

By the time Johnny Boy returned, in the late afternoon to beat the descending darkness, Ricketts and his men had seen a lot of military traffic passing both ways on the MSR below the ridge, though nothing that looked like a genuine Scud launcher. What they *did* see on the MSR were mobile Scud decoys, constructed in East Germany, complete with their own crews, only there to draw the fire of Coalition aircraft and encourage the pilots to submit false 'kill' reports.

'When I think I'm having it rough,' Jock said, 'I'll bless the fates for not making me do *that* job. What a way to go!'

'Better than getting cancer,' Paddy replied. 'Even better than AIDS. One little shell, a big bang, and it's all over before you even know it. I'd *kill* for that fucking job!'

When Johnny Boy got back – 'in time for supper', as he put it – he told them that the Scud mobile launchers were avoiding the MSRs and instead using old dirt tracks to cross the desert and evade the AWACS aircraft.

'I found two separate bunkers,' he told them, wolfing down his cold food and water. 'I've marked their positions on my maps. They're the same as the Iraqi hardened aircraft shelters: pyramid-shaped and flat-roofed, with sliding steel doors, half buried in heaped-up earth and sand to make them blend in with the desert. The mobile Scud launchers are huge, raised up on the backs of wheeled platforms towed by trucks. They're usually accompanied by a truck filled with armed troops, but they'd be pretty easy to take out. Just slam them with Stingers or MILANs while raking the troops with GPMGs. Piece of piss, boss.'

Carefully covering up the OP, Ricketts and the rest went out that same night in the Pink Panthers and LSVs, led by Johnny Boy on his Honda. First, he led them to the two bunkers, located about fifteen miles apart. The exact locations of the bunkers were then relayed by SATCOM to HQ in Riyadh. Those messages were relayed in turn to the US Tactical Aircraft Control Centre, from there to an AWACS aircraft, and thence to an F-15E already in the air on nocturnal combat patrol.

While the F-15E was en route to the bunker, Ricketts and his team illuminated the target with large, camera-like laser designators mounted on tripods. Having done this, they used the cover of darkness to quietly plant small, disposable transmitters around the bunker, jamming its communications and preventing it from radar-tracking the incoming attack plane.

At both locations the aircraft arrived within

half an hour of the original SATCOM message being relayed.

When the plane released its GBU-15 laser-guided bombs just ahead of the grid location received from the men on the ground, the bombs, homing in on the intense spot of light 'painted' on the bunkers by the designators, were directed with pinpoint accuracy through their open doors or, in the second case, an open window.

Blown to hell from inside, the bunkers belched flame, smoke and debris before collapsing in billowing clouds of sand and dust. Ricketts and his men then approached the site by foot, checking that the launchers had been taken out and that the members of the Scud teams were dead. The answer in both cases, at both locations, was brutally affirmative.

By the second day, after another grim night in the OP, with worsening weather, including alternating bouts of sleet, snow, hail and frost, Ricketts and his men, taking note of Hailsham's changed attitude and sharing his frustration, were patrolling the whole area in daylight and coming across many mobile Scud units. Soon learning that it took fifteen minutes or more for an aircraft to arrive on target and that often, in the case of a mobile launcher, this was too late, they began taking matters into their own hands. Rather than see a Scud escape, they blew it to hell with their Stinger or MILAN anti-tank missiles while massacring the accompanying troops with relentless fire from their machine-guns, M16s and SLRs.

Such attacks were made either from the weapons mounted on parked, camouflaged vehicles or from the LSV as it raced towards the convoy, its MILAN firing on the move. Even as the MILAN shells were tearing into the Scud launcher, causing it to explode with a mighty roar, the LSV would be swerving sideways and haring alongside the convoy, followed by the Pink Panther, thus enabling the GPMGs and small arms of Ricketts, Jock and Paddy – Andrew was driving the LSV, Danny the Pink Panther – to rake the surprised Iraqi troops with murderous fire.

Usually Johnny Boy would accompany the LSV and Pink Panther on their daring run around the Scud convoy, recklessly guiding his Honda with one hand while firing his Browning pistol with the other, rarely getting off his 13 shots without taking out at least a few Iraqis. Then the Pink Panther, LSV and motorbike would race away in churning clouds of sand even before the debris from the exploding Scud launcher had stopped raining down upon the dazed, dead or dying enemy soldiers. It was a dance of death on bullet-riddled desert sands, conducted with ruthless efficiency.

Over the next three days, encouraged by success, Ricketts and his men started going for the weak spots in Saddam's whole communications system, hitting microwave relay towers and communications bunkers, blowing them up where they were located, either along the MSRs or by the highway that ran between Baghdad and Amman. What they could not destroy with their Stingers, MILANs or plastic explosives, they smashed with sledgehammers.

The appalling weather was worsening, and despite their heavily padded jerkins and cloaks, the men were suffering even more from sleet, hail, frost and occasional snow. Two or three times during the night they had to light fires beneath their Land Rovers to prevent the diesel fuel from freezing. By the fourth night, fog and sand storms were added to their problems, so they were greatly relieved when, on the fifth day, they were able to pack up their gear, fill in their OPs and drive back to be resupplied, debriefed and reunited with the other patrols at the Wadi Tubal rendezvous, still inside Iraq.

The SAS ran its own supply column overland. This consisted of ten four-ton trucks crewed by badged SAS soldiers and REME mechanics, escorted by teams drawn from B Squadron in six armed Land Rovers. The caravan was led by an eccentric captain who informed Major Hailsham that his attacks on the Scud launchers had been successful, driving them further and further into the Iraqi hinterland, all but out of range of Israel and Saudi Arabia.

'The danger of Israel entering the war has receded,' the captain said, 'so you're now free to look for a wider variety of targets. The green slime has suggested radar sites, petroleum refineries, storage tanks and ammunition depots. Go to it, Major.'

When Hailsham conveyed this information to his Lurp teams, they celebrated their success by decorating their vehicles with stencilled silhouettes of individual kills, in the shape of Scud launchers and communications towers.

Over the next five days a mobile workshop was kept busy as more SAS columns came in from the Scud box. Entire engines were replaced, tyres, brakes and suspension were checked, weapons were stripped and serviced, and lost kit was replaced. Then Hailsham called his men together for another briefing.

'Having sussed from our raids that we're in the area,' he said, 'the Iraqis are bound to try hunting us down. So life in Scud Alley is going to be more dangerous from now on.'

Having given his men this grim warning, he then issued new orders, which naturally involved even deeper penetration of Scud Alley.

'We leave tomorrow,' he told them.

7

The plan was to position road-watch patrols overlooking the three MSRs that ran from the crowded Euphrates Valley up a vast desert slope to the Jordanian hills in the west. These were foot patrols. RAF Chinooks put down the three separate SAS groups – known as Road Watch North, Centre and South – about twenty miles apart on a north-south axis.

The most isolated of the teams inserted, Road Watch North, was dropped in the middle of the night in rocky terrain swept by a howling, freezing wind and pouring rain – not quite what they had expected in the desert. Though they unloaded their bergens and weapons as quickly as possible, they were still drenched even before the helicopter took off again and they could huddle in the nearest shelter available, near the head of a dry, dead-end wadi about fifteen feet deep. The wind was so strong, it practically drowned out the clamour of the departing chopper.

'Christ!' Taff exclaimed as he dropped his bergen to the ground between his raised knees and wrapped his arms around his shivering body. 'This is worse than the Falklands!'

'Yeah, right,' Geordie replied, wiping rain from his eyes and checking the waterproof wrapping around the PRC 319 radio system. 'I thought it was supposed to be a fucking desert.'

'It *is* desert,' Andrew said, glancing about him in bewilderment. 'It's just not *hot* desert. There's a lot of rock and gravel in this area and the weather's shit-awful.'

'Lots of rain, sleet and snow,' Ricketts explained. 'You'll get no suntan here.' Raising his head to peer over the rim of the wadi, squinting against the driving rain, he saw only flat terrain with the dark outline of a ridge a few hundred yards away, outlined against a black sky. No moon or stars out there. The wind was howling across the flat land, driving the rain before it. 'It looks like hell on earth out there. We couldn't have picked a worse night.'

'I want to go home already,' Andrew said. 'Where's the nearest friendly territory?'

'About a hundred and eighty-odd miles away.'

'I'll stay here,' Andrew said.

Geordie laughed sardonically as he unwrapped the covering of netting and hessian required for the OP. 'We'll fucking stay here all right. There's nowhere else to go. So we might as well put a roof over our heads and keep the rain out before this wadi turns into a swamp.' Even as he spoke, he received an incoming transmission signal on the PRC 319. After switching on the receiver and listening to the message, he handed the microphone to Ricketts. 'Road Watch South,' he explained.

Through an inordinate amount of static created by the storm, Ricketts just about heard the voice of Major Hailsham, who had insisted on being the commander of the road watch nearest the Saudi border. Now he was explaining over the radio that he had decided to go back to the FOB.

'The terrain of this LZ's completely featureless,' he said, 'and much too exposed to be useful. If we stay here, we'll be sitting ducks for the Iraqis, so I'm calling the chopper back. Road Watch Centre might be having similar problems. How's it with you?'

'It's too early to say,' Ricketts responded. 'The combination of storm and darkness makes it difficult to see, so we'll stay here at least until the morning.'

'Read you, Sergeant-Major. Good luck. Over and out.'

'He's got good sense,' Geordie said when Ricketts had handed the microphone back.

'That's why he's an officer,' Andrew said, 'and you're still a mere trooper. Come on, guys, let's sort out this OP before we're all washed away.'

'Good idea,' Danny said.

Mercifully, the rain passed on a few minutes later and the howling wind gradually settled down to an eerie moan. While not a great comfort, this made it easier for the men to construct the OP with a camouflaged roof of netting, waterproof canvas, hessian and sand, as well as plastic sheeting to cover the waterlogged bottom of the wadi. It was long, narrow, cold and damp, but it was enough to be going on with, at least until morning broke.

What happened tomorrow would depend entirely on what they found when they could see the terrain. Right now, cold and damp, with the wind howling eerily, Ricketts, thinking of Hailsham's departure, was suffering an unaccustomed feeling of isolation.

That disquiet was increased when, shortly after

the completion of the OP, he received another radio message, this time from the commander of Road Watch Centre, stating that his LZ was on flat, moon-like terrain where concealment was virtually impossible.

'We're bugging out,' he said. 'Making a tactical withdrawal. As a parting shot, however, I'm going to call down an A10 air strike on the two enemy mobile radar systems I can see from right here. I'll keep you informed of events right up to the moment we actually leave. Over and out.'

The A10s duly arrived and were lined up on the target when the commander of Road Watch Centre realized that his LZ was being mistaken for the target. Immediately, he sent a radio signal to tactical HQ but the signal was not received. According to the next message received by Ricketts, the air attack destroyed the Iraqi radar and only narrowly missed the troopers who had called it up.

Ricketts and his men witnessed the air strike from ten miles away: another spectacular light show of crimson tracers, silvery explosions and fire-spewing missiles illuminating the night sky, accompanied by the distant thunder of explosions. When it ended, Ricketts received another message from the commander, saying they had nearly been bombed by their own planes, but at least the Iraqi positions had been destroyed. The commander then confirmed that his team was bugging out, making a hasty, controlled exit from the LZ by foot.

Ricketts wished him well, then cut communications, realizing with foreboding that his group, Road Watch North, was now completely on its own, 187 miles from friendly territory.

That thought chilled him as much as did the biting wind and the dark, damp earth around him.

Huddled up in their OP, the patrol spent a miserable first night, supposedly watching for the movement of Scud launchers along the nearby MSR, but in fact unable to see anything beyond a hundred yards or so. The weather remained bitterly cold, with temperatures well below freezing throughout the night, accompanied by gusts of driving wind, rain, sleet and snow. Ricketts was only too aware that it was weather similar to that which had often killed soldiers and civilians on the SAS training ground of Brecon Beacons.

Raising his head again, just before the break of dawn, he checked that the desert immediately around them was indeed flat rock, rising gently to a ridge about two hundred yards to the north.

It was. In the fading darkness he could see the ridge more clearly, outlined against a sky now showing patches of stars, with what appeared to be an angular rock formation on its low summit. The OP itself was located in a wadi running along the crest of a hill that fell away behind them and to the side. The terrain in front of them was flat for about four hundred yards, and then it, too, started falling away to the plain below. That plain was criss-crossed by the parallel lines of the MSRs about five miles away. All in all, it was a mountainous, rocky area, splashed here and there with white patches of snow, ice and frost. The wind blew all the time.

Eventually, to his despair, even before the dawn broke properly, Ricketts realized that what had appeared to be a rock formation was actually two Iraqi S60 anti-aircraft gun positions on top of the ridge overlooking his OP.

'Shit!' he hissed involuntarily.

'What's that, boss?' Andrew asked, removing the binoculars from his eyes after scanning the MSRs on the low desert plain to the west.

Ricketts said nothing. He merely pointed at the nearby ridge with his index finger.

'Oh, man!' Andrew sighed when he saw the Iraqi gun positions. 'We is in bad trouble, man!'

One by one the other men in the OP, some of whom had been sleeping, turned their heads to look up at the ridge and murmur their own version of despair.

There was no way to get out of the OP without being seen.

'We're trapped here,' Ricketts said.

'Christ!' Taff burst out, gazing up at the ridge with disbelief in his sleepless, bloodshot eyes. 'What the hell do we do?'

Ricketts wasn't sure, but he had to say something. 'We'll just have to sit tight and hope to hell something turns up.'

'What might that be, boss?'

As Danny rarely spoke, the question was well worth considering. But no immediate answer came to Ricketts. 'I don't know. I only know we can't move. Let's just do as much as we can while we're here. For a start, take notes on those anti-aircraft gun emplacements, then the movements of enemy aircraft or any activity on the ground, including those distant MSRs. What's happening there, Andrew?'

'Whoever picked this location for an OP,' Andrew replied, speaking with his binoculars to his eyes, 'ought to be hung, drawn and quartered – the slower the better. Those MSRs are a good five miles away and covered in fog. I can't see shit, boss.'

'The fog will disappear as the sun rises. Keep looking, Sergeant.'

A grey dawn led into an interminable day whose monotony was only broken for the individual men by a period on watch, a turn at domestic chores, sleep, then another period of watch. Even with the sunlight, the temperature scarcely rose above freezing point. Added to this torture was the boredom, relieved only by the military traffic passing along the distant MSR or the passage of aircraft, both Coalition and Iraqi, on their way to and from Baghdad or Basra. Notes on all these movements were duly recorded, but the men still felt trapped.

To make matters worse, radio transmissions to HQ were less than perfect. 'On HF,' Geordie informed Ricketts, 'I'm losing words and sometimes whole sentences. It's not helpful, boss.' Nevertheless, by the end of the first day Geordie had heard enough on high-frequency transmissions to be able to inform Ricketts that there was no news of the missing members of Road Watch Centre, who had bugged out of their LZ on foot. By now, Ricketts thought, they were either dead, wounded, captured or committing daring acts of espionage. It was best not to dwell on it.

Occasionally they heard sounds of human activity – a dog barking, goatherds calling to each other only a hundred yards away – sounds telling them that neither they nor the Iraqi soldiers on the ridge were completely alone in this vast, inhospitable wilderness.

Ricketts was still racking his brains over how to get out of this trap when, at sunset, with the mist again creeping over the flat, gravelly earth in front of the OP, the goatherds materialized over the crest of the slope 300 yards away. They were wearing the customary headcloth, the *keffia*, draped over their head and shoulders, and the *dish-disha*, a plain, one-piece shirt reaching from the throat to the feet. Their feet were in leather thongs. Urging the goats ahead of them with the aid of gnarled sticks and a couple of undernourished dogs, they were coming directly towards the OP. Ricketts counted four men.

Immediately, without a word, the SAS troopers placed themselves in firing positions along the OP, some of them aiming at the goatherds, others preparing to fire on the ridge should their position be given away to the gun crews. Luckily the dogs cut alongside the advancing goats, raced around in front of them and turned them back the way they had come.

'Thank Christ for that,' Taff whispered.

Ricketts, however, was certain that one of the goatherds, who had turned away with the goats but then turned back to stare quizzically at the raised earth around the OP, had actually seen it.

Whether or not he would tell someone later on remained to be seen. For the moment, he simply turned away and, as the evening descended, followed his animals and fellow goatherds down the far slope.

Ricketts heaved a sigh of relief.

'Close one,' Andrew said.

Another interminable evening and a hellishly cold, damp night had to be endured. The men could neither leave the OP to relieve themselves nor take a chance on leaving the OP altogether, in case the goatherd, who had possibly seen them, informed on them, in which case the Iraqi soldiers on the ridge would be waiting to ambush them.

When no movement on the part of the Iraqis was made by noon the second day, Ricketts resolved to try to bluff his way out. He was confirmed in this decision when the Arabs returned with their animals and the goatherd he suspected of having seen the OP looked only briefly in its direction. If the man had seen the OP – and Ricketts thought he had – he might be friendly to the Coalition forces. Either that, or he was wrongly assuming that the OP was part of the military operation being conducted by the Iraqi soldiers on the ridge. As either way the goats were going to reach the OP, thus exposing the position, Ricketts decided to try his bluff.

'Put on your *shemaghs*,' he instructed his men, 'and keep your mouths shut. I can speak a little Arabic, so let me do the talking.'

When he and the other men had put on their veils to hide their faces, Ricketts stood up in full view and tried waving in a friendly way at the Iraqi goatherds. Even if they turned out to be unfriendly, it was possible that with the *shemaghs* covering the berets and faces of the SAS troopers, the goatherds would mistake them for Iraqi troops and either ignore their presence or let them march off.

However, even as Ricketts was waving, the goatherds, looking uneasy, went off to the side again, disappearing down the rocky, frost-covered slope. At that moment a self-sustaining Iraqi unit with its command vehicle and tracked carriers arrived, braking to a halt about three hundred yards away.

As Ricketts ducked low, hardly believing what was happening, the canvas covers were whipped off the trucks and a battery of low-level anti-aircraft guns was revealed. The men in the trucks jumped out. Some of them made a camp-fire and started boiling soup or tea. Others made their way up to the ridge, to talk to the men in the gun emplacements.

Obviously the site chosen for the SAS OP was one that had also been chosen by the Iraqis as part of their rapidly growing air-defence network.

'Jesus Christ,' Andrew whispered, 'I think I'm having a bad dream!'

'I wish you were,' Ricketts replied. Determined to keep his wits together, he immediately sent a short-burst message over the SATCOM system, stating that an enemy triple-A gun was in position immediately north of the LZ. The terse reply was that the close proximity of the Iraqis made relief, resupply or rescue by air impossible, for to call down fire on the enemy would be to virtually attract the same to their own position. Unfortunately, they would have to sit tight and hope that the Iraqis would disappear, sooner or later.

'Fucking terrific,' Geordie said, replacing the microphone. 'We could be here for ever.'

'Even if we get out,' Taff asked, 'where the hell could we go?'

'Let's try taking them out,' Danny urged, itching for action. 'We've got nothing to lose.'

'Only our lives,' Ricketts replied. 'I say we sit tight, wait for that mobile unit to leave, then take our chances on getting out under cover of darkness, when the men on the ridge may not see us.'

'They may not leave for days,' Andrew said. 'They're settling in over there.'

'Let's wait, Andrew. Let's see.'

Unable to leave, they had to piss and shit in the OP, favouring the far end of the wadi, which eased neither the humiliation nor the stench. They were also running short of food and water. After another night huddled up in the cold, damp, narrow OP, fearful of sleeping in case the Iraqis came their way, they were not only close to serious exhaustion, but also in danger of contracting hypothermia.

'I say we get up and run,' Andrew suggested. 'Take our chances out there. We can't stay here much longer, boss.'

'Right,' Danny agreed, his finger itchy on the

trigger. 'Even if we don't have a chance, we can take some of them out with us.'

'No,' Ricketts replied. 'The men in that mobile unit packed up their plates and saucers this morning, so I think they'll leave soon. If they do, we'll stay here until this evening, then move out under cover of darkness.'

'Fucking right,' Geordie said.

Unfortunately their luck ran out. About noon that day, the third day, they saw the goatherd being driven in a jeep to the mobile unit and being deposited in front of an Iraqi officer. After words were exchanged, the Iraqi officer slapped the goatherd's face, threw him to the ground, kicked him viciously and then stared in the direction of the OP.

'Shit!' Ricketts exclaimed. 'The goatherd's told them about us.'

The OP was filled with the metallic clatter of weapons being brought into position as the Iraqi officer and some soldiers from the mobile group clambered hurriedly into a jeep and drove towards the OP.

Andrew opened fire with his GPMG, firing a sustained burst that peppered the jeep with noisily ricocheting 7.62mm bullets, bursting its front tyres and hitting the driver, who shook like a rag doll and released the steering wheel as his grey tunic was splashed with red. The men on either side of Andrew also opened fire as the jeep skidded sideways, exposing the men in the rear to a hail of bullets from the M16s and SLRs. The Iraqis were throwing their hands up and crying out with pain even as the rear tyres burst and the jeep rolled onto its side. When Andrew fired a burst into its petrol tank, it burst into flames. The men still alive, or simply wounded by the hail of bullets, screamed hideously as they were incinerated in the pyre of the blazing jeep.

At that moment a mortar shell exploded just in front of the OP, creating a thunderous din and a fountain of spewing earth that rained back down on Ricketts and his men.

'They're shooting at us from the gun emplacements on the ridge!' Danny shouted as another mortar shell exploded, filling the air with smoke and flying gravel, followed immediately by the stitching effects of machine-gun fire from the mobile unit 300 yards away.

'Get in touch with HQ!' Ricketts bawled to Geordie. 'Tell them we're bugging out and need covering fire!'

'I'm trying,' Geordie called back, 'but I'm not

getting through! The reception keeps fading in and out! We've got faulty transmission!'

Ricketts glanced out of the OP as the smoke from the mortar explosions drifted away and gave him a clear view once more. The exploded jeep was still blazing, but the men inside it were now silent, blackened, smouldering corpses. Beyond them, the remaining Iraqis of the mobile unit were passing weapons to one another in preparation for an assault on the OP. Another mortar shell exploded, fired from the distant ridge. This one landed even closer to the OP, making the ground shake, practically deafening the men, filling the air with acrid smoke and obscuring the view again.

'Stow your survival gear in your bergens,' Ricketts instructed his men, 'and let's get the hell out of here. We're in for a very long march, so don't take anything heavy.'

'I'm taking my GPMG,' Andrew insisted.

'You're a big boy,' Ricketts said with a grin, 'and you're the one who'll be carrying it. OK, let's bug out!'

The men clambered, heavily laden, out of the OP and made their way downhill as the first fusillade of fire came from the remaining Iraqi soldiers. Using any fold in the ground

113

available, Ricketts's men fired back as they moved off.

Surprised, the Iraqis paused, then started shooting with renewed vigour with their small arms. As they did so, the soldiers behind them, on the trailer-truck, used the triple-A anti-aircraft guns on a low trajectory, thus converting the heavy-calibre guns into deadly infantry-support weapons.

Mere seconds after the last SAS trooper, Danny Porter, had clambered out of the OP and raced to catch up with the others, the gun crews on the ridge finally got an accurate calibration and two mortar shells blew the empty OP apart.

As the Iraqi troops advanced through the swirling smoke and raining gravel, bullets from their small arms stitched the ground around the SAS men, noisily ricocheting off rocks and sending stones flying in all directions. At the same time, shells from the triple-A anti-aircraft guns, as well as the mortars on the ridge, made the ground behind them erupt in a series of deafening explosions that spewed earth, gravel, sand and pieces of razor-sharp, burning shrapnel.

Ricketts felt himself being picked up in a roaring maelstrom, his breath sucked from scorched lungs, before he was whipped over once or twice and smashed back down to earth. His head was filled with a whistling sound and white light seared the darkness, but he managed to spit sand from his mouth and open his eyes again. He was flat on his back with smoke drifting above him. When he rolled over and pushed himself up on hands and knees, most of the contents of his bergen fell out, clattering noisily on the frosted gravel beneath him.

'A piece of shrapnel slashed your bergen,' Danny explained, grabbing Ricketts under the shoulder and helping him back to his feet, 'but you look OK, Sarge.'

'That shrapnel also damaged my radio,' Geordie said. 'Now it's completely fucking useless. You ask me, boss, I think we should ditch the bergens anyway. We've got a long walk ahead and the bergens are too heavy to carry.'

His ears still ringing, Ricketts glanced back the way he had come. Having reached the smouldering OP on the crest of the hill, the Iraqi troops were advancing around it and coming on down, firing their small arms on the march. The triple-A anti-aircraft guns had finally stopped firing, but the mortar on the ridge was still in action, its shells coming closer.

'OK,' Ricketts said. 'We're outnumbered and

outgunned. We'll have to leg it out of here. Ditch the bergens, radio and everything else except your weapons, water bottles and spare ammo. Keep what food you have left and your personal rescue beacons. Let's be quick about it. Andrew, keep those bastards away from us until we bug out.'

'Right, boss. Will do.' An impressively big man, Andrew handled the GPMG as if it was a lightweight toy. Instead of fixing it to the tripod – he didn't have the time anyway – he spread his strong legs, crooked the heavy weapon in one arm, and fired from the hip, his whole body shaking with the recoil as he moved the barrel left and right to spray in a broad arc. The noise was atrocious, but the burst of fire was deadly, bowling over many of the Iraqis and making the others scatter, throw themselves to the ground or race back up the hill to take cover in the still smouldering OP.

As the rest of the SAS troopers divested themselves of their bergens, taking only the bare essentials, they joined Andrew in keeping the Iraqis pinned down, by firing with their small arms. When the last of them had ditched his bergen and was ready to leave, they walked away backwards, firing from the hip for as long as required. Once out of range of the Iraqi gunfire, they turned away, spreading farther apart, and ran as fast as they could across the flat plain sweeping out from the bottom of the hill to the distant horizon.

The Iraqis, they knew, would follow cautiously. But follow they certainly would.

8

A few hours after legging it out of the OP, the men stopped for a rest in another hilly, rocky area that had emerged out of the flat plain just as a hazy-white sun was sinking over the darkening horizon. Just as it became completely dark, they saw the headlights of several vehicles following them.

'They're still on our tail,' Ricketts said, 'and won't stop till they catch us.'

'The night at least offers us some protection,' Andrew observed, 'so I say we keep moving, boss.'

Danny glanced around him, seeing nothing but a vast, flat plain with low hills in the distance. 'Which direction?' he asked.

Ricketts checked his map by the light of a pencil torch. 'Urbanized Iraq is to the east, so that way offers only certain capture. Westward is Jordan, a non-combatant ally of Saddam Hussein. As they've already handed over a downed American pilot to the Iraqis, I don't think they'll treat us any better.' He glanced up from the map and gazed south at the lights of the Iraqi troop trucks following them. 'That's south, so obviously we can't go there. Which leaves north. Or, more accurately, north-west and the frontier with Syria – a member of the anti-Iraqi coalition. We might be OK there.'

'*If* we get there,' Geordie said. 'It's a hell of a hike.'

'Any other ideas?' Andrew asked.

'Nope,' Geordie replied.

'Then north-west it is.' Andrew also glanced at the lights advancing far to the south. 'And I say we go now.'

'Let's try to shake those bastards off our tail,' Ricketts said. 'First, by going south, then a short leg to the west, then on a northerly heading, which will eventually lead us back to the north-westerly stretch of the MSR. If we follow that, while keeping clear of it, we should reach the border.'

Andrew flashed his perfect teeth in a broad grin. 'If any of you have prayers say them now, before you run out of breath.'

'Very funny, Sergeant,' Geordie said. 'We're all in fits. Can we walk and not talk?'

'Read you loud and clear, Geordie.'

'OK,' Ricketts said, 'let's go.'

Steering by compass, and with the help of their SATNAV global positioning system, they started off again, finding it easier without the heavy bergens, but not thrilled by the sight of that endless plain running out to the low hills on the horizon. The vehicles behind them had stopped moving, as they could see by the lights, which probably meant that the Iraqis had disembarked to search that particular area. It was a good sign. They would have to do that a lot. Which, in turn, would give the SAS troopers on foot the possibility of staying well ahead.

Without even thinking about it, they had fallen into file formation, with Danny well out front, taking the 'point' as lead scout and constantly checking what lay ahead through the infrared night-sight of his rifle. The others were strung out behind him, a good distance apart, maintaining irregular spaces between them to avoid unnecessary, or too many, casualties if attacked.

Marching behind Danny, Ricketts, as PC, was second in line, with Geordie, as signaller, though now without his radio, and Taff bringing up the rear as 'Tail-end Charlie'. While this was undoubtedly the safest method for this kind of march, it did not allow for conversation or any other time-passing activities, which in turn made them even more conscious of the distance, and therefore more tired.

Contributing to the latter problem was the fact that although they were blessedly free of their heavy bergens, they were still burdened with personal kit belts laden with basic survival gear, items of first aid, water bottles, emergency rations, spare ammunition, and smoke and fragmentation grenades. These alone made for a weight that would have broken most men's back on a hike such as this. Last but not least was the mentally exhausting need for constant vigilance, particularly with regard to minefields, which could have been anywhere and would, if they existed, be particularly hard to see in this wind-blown darkness.

The wind, both chilling and eerie, constantly blew sand and dust across the plain, covering up small rocks that could trip them, wadis into which they might inadvertently fall, and, worst of all, obscuring any minefields that might be there.

Should they come across a minefield, Danny,

out front on point, would almost certainly be the first to 'beat the clock'. He knew that, but he didn't give a damn – he always wanted to be first into the fray. Though remarkably youthful and still called 'Baby Face', Danny continued to be widely viewed by the other troopers as a natural soldier and killer. Out on point, the most dangerous place, was where he belonged.

After marching the men southwards for two and a half hours, or about twelve miles, Ricketts checked their location with his hand-held SATNAV GPS, then led them west for another six miles. This took them from flat desert to more rocky terrain, where the moonlight glinted on patches of ice and the wind whipped up snowflakes.

Feeling protected by the hills, they stopped for a break at the end of the twelve-mile stretch, some drinking the last of their water, others nibbling on barely edible dried food. Occasionally aircraft flew overhead, but in the darkness they could not make out if they were friend or foe. The wind howled constantly, blowing sand and dust around them, and the cold was eating at their bones, sinking in, taking hold.

'I feel exhausted already,' Taff said, 'and we

haven't even come very far. I don't know what's wrong with me.'

'Cold and lack of food,' Andrew said. 'More the cold than the food. The cold makes you feel tired.'

'I think my feet are blistered,' Geordie said, 'but I can't even feel them. Fucking numb, they are.'

'Better your feet than your cock,' Andrew said.

'That's numb as well.'

'Oh, boy, you is in trouble! Now you've nothing to pull on. Me? When I start feeling exhausted, I just pull on my big dong and think of England. That keeps me going.'

'It keeps you coming,' Geordie corrected him.

'I never cream my jeans,' Andrew retorted. 'I think it's bad manners.'

'Hey, Moorcock!' Geordie said, again moved by the impulse to stir a little shit with the probationers. 'Do you think it's bad manners to cream your jeans or do you stick to pyjamas?'

Trooper Moorcock, even though visibly exhausted, blushed a deep, virginal crimson. 'Gee, Geordie . . . I mean . . . Hey, come on, I don't have to . . . What I mean,' he said, struggling for an answer, 'is that I don't . . . I just *don't*.'

'Low sperm count?' Andrew asked.

'What?'

'Never mind.'

'He wouldn't know it if he had it in his hand,' Geordie said with a big grin. 'That's innocence for you.'

'Leave him alone,' Trooper Stone said, starting to understand this ritual. 'You guys are just trying to embarrass him. Now me, I have a high sperm count and it's in my hand quite a lot.'

'It's good for the complexion,' Taff managed, though his voice sounded shaky. 'At least that's what my women say.'

'What women?' Geordie asked. 'I've never seen you with a woman. That's why you're always wiping the sperm count off your fingers when you think we're not looking.'

'What does that mean?' Trooper Gillett asked, exhausted, confused and uneasy, wondering what the next hour would bring and starting to dread it.

'He's a bachelor,' Andrew explained. 'He doesn't have it on tap. When he wants it, he either buys an expensive meal for some tart or saves costs by going to bed with *Playboy*. His fingers often get tired though.'

'You filthy bastard,' Taff croaked.

'I'm not a bastard,' Andrew replied.

'I never know what you blokes are talking about,' Trooper Moorcock said, sounding strained, glancing down at his feet, and shivering helplessly. 'Why don't you talk English?'

'Those bastards are still coming after us,' Taff said, sounding breathless and hoarse.

When they looked back, across the immense, dark plain, they saw those familiar lights in the distance, on the move again.

'Come on,' Ricketts urged. 'Let's get going.'

They changed direction once more, this time onto a northerly heading, marching as quickly as they could, which was not as quick as before, trying to put more distance between themselves and the Iraqis behind them.

The moaning wind grew in strength, and snow began to fall. Frost was breaking under their desert boots and freezing their feet. The wind was biting and blew sand around them. Though they all had veils over their faces and tinted glasses protecting their eyes, the mixture of cutting sand and freezing snow was a further menace that had to be accepted.

The march seemed interminable and was thoroughly debilitating, a murderous combination of howling wind, freezing snow, biting sand, loneliness and the constant, exhausting need to beware of minefields, all the while keeping an eye on the Iraqis still in hot pursuit. The lights were right there behind them, advancing slowly but surely, still in the distance only because the Iraqi soldiers were constantly criss-crossing the desert, leaving no stone unturned. They were, however, gradually gaining distance and closing the gap.

As all the SAS men knew that they would, if captured, be treated with more than the usual harshness, they were given further impetus to keep moving, though the toll was now telling. Twice Taff tripped and fell, which was an indication of lack of attention brought on by exhaustion. This knowledge made Ricketts more uneasy.

By the time they got back to the MSR it was midnight. Already they had walked for seven hours and covered some forty miles. While the men had another short break, squatting on the windswept sand and drinking the last of their water, Ricketts surveyed the MSR through his night-vision binoculars. At one point, he noticed, it was one or two miles wide, a dangerously flat, open stretch, with dozens of tracks side by side, spread out across the desert. On rechecking, however, he realized that the MSR had made a sweeping curve not shown on the map and that their escape route now lay across that series of Iraqi-controlled, parallel desert tracks.

'That's pretty fucking hairy,' Geordie observed. 'It's wide-open out there.'

'Right,' Andrew agreed. 'And once we start crossing, we'll be completely exposed, with the likelihood of Iraqi military convoys coming along. Bloody dangerous, boss.'

'We've no choice,' Ricketts said. 'Either we take that chance or we sit here and let those bastards on our tail catch up with us. One advantage is that this damned wind that's been driving us mad is sweeping the sand and snow across the MSR, sometimes obscuring it. That should give us at least some protection. Also, the terrain at the far side is hilly, so if we can manage to get that far without being caught, we'll have more cover than we have here. Still, you're right, it could be hairy. It's a collective decision, men, but I say we keep going.'

The men automatically looked back at the lights of the trucks on their tail, then across the parallel tracks of the MSR, placed a good distance apart on another flat, featureless desert plain along which Iraqi military traffic was known to travel. It was a choice between a rock and a hard place, and all of them knew it.

'What about you, Taff?' Ricketts asked, nervous about his condition.

'Don't ask me,' Taff replied without the slightest trace of irony. 'I'm too exhausted to even think about it. To be honest, I'm not sure I can make it. I'm sorry. That's how I feel.'

'He's exhausted,' Danny said. 'There's no question about it. It's probably due to the cold more than the march, but either way he's in bad shape.'

'I say we take his kit and weapons off him,' the nervous, but decent, Trooper Moorcock suggested, 'and put him behind Danny in the file formation. That way we can watch him.'

'Can I take it from those statements,' Ricketts asked, 'that you're all in favour of going on?'

'Yes, boss.'

'Me, too,' Geordie said.

'Fucked if I'm going to stay here and have my fingernails pulled out by Iraqi pliers,' Andrew added sardonically. 'Let's do it, boss.'

'What about you men?' Ricketts asked the probationers, troopers Moorcock, Gillett and Stone.

'I'm with you,' Stone said.

'Me, too,' Gillett said.

Moorcock stared at his two friends, glanced at the others one by one, stared across the dark plain at the advancing lights of the Iraqi trucks, then turned back to Ricketts and nodded his agreement.

'Right,' Ricketts said. 'Divide Taff's kit and weapons between you and let's bug out of here.'

The men did as they were told, relieving the grateful Taff of his burden, then Danny headed off, Taff fell in behind him and the others took their places one by one, well apart in the standard file formation, following Danny down the slope to the desert plain and the wind-blown tracks of the MSR.

Still protecting their rear, Ricketts glanced back over his shoulder just before starting down the rocky slope. The lights of the Iraqi trucks were now dangerously close and the trucks were clearly picking up speed. Obviously the soldiers had realized that their quarry was not on the plain and that the MSR would have to be crossed. There was not much time left.

Ricketts hurried down the slope, following the others. Once out of the protection of the rocks, they were exposed to the full force of the wind and the fiercely swirling, stinging sand

and freezing snow. The blowing sand gave them cover, obscuring the bright stars, but was so dense that they had to close up, in case they lost sight of one another.

By the time they reached the MSR, or at least its first track, they were half blinded by the sand, frozen numb by the snow and not sure if they were heading in the right direction.

Danny looked left and right, checking the track's alignment, then raised his right hand and waved them on, stepping out in the lead. As they crossed the MSR, going from one track to the next, with sometimes a quarter of a mile between them, the sound of gunfire exploded behind them and bullets whipped past.

'They're right behind us!' Ricketts bawled.

Danny glanced back over his shoulder just as Ricketts turned away and fired his SLR at the headlamps beaming dimly through the gloom from approximately the first track of the MSR. One of the lights blinked out, obviously damaged by Ricketts's gunfire, but the others were moving inexorably forward, though mercifully at a snail's pace, because the sweeping sand and snow were blinding the drivers. Ricketts fired a second burst and another set of lights blinked out, but a fusillade of return fire from the trucks made sand and snow spurt viciously from the flat ground about him.

'Spread out and keep going!' Ricketts bawled.

'Give me a weapon!' Taff cried out to Danny.

'No!' Danny said. 'Run!'

He hared off across the next track, almost disappearing in the murk, and was followed by Taff and the others. Ricketts, protecting their rear, hurled a phosphorus grenade at the approaching lights, then dropped to one knee and continued firing. He was soon joined by Moorcock, Stone and Gillett, all firing as well.

The grenade exploded with a shocking roar, filling the darkness with an immense fountain of white flames, streaming fireflies of silvery phosphorus, swirling black smoke and billowing clouds of sand. The deafening roar of the explosion was followed by the screams of the wounded.

Geordie joined Ricketts and the other three, firing his M16 in rapid bursts, even as Danny reached the far side of the MSR and turned back to see what was happening. He saw Geordie drop to one knee beside Ricketts, both in the firing position and erratically illuminated in the silvery light of the explosion, just before the raining sand and swirling smoke obscured them completely.

SOLDIER A: SAS

Taff and Andrew burst out of the murk as
Ricketts and Geordie disappeared.

'Let's get into the hills,' Danny said, 'and hope
they catch up. That's what Ricketts wanted.'

'Yeah, let's go,' Andrew growled.

Another grenade exploded behind them, followed by gunfire from both sides, and the silvery
flames and fireflies created by phosphorus briefly
illuminated the stormy darkness as Andrew,
Danny and Taff climbed up into the relative
safety of the hills.

Once in the shelter of the lower slopes,
surrounded by rocky outcroppings, they sat
down and waited. But although the moving
lights showed that the Iraqi trucks had turned
back, there was no sign of the other SAS men.
The fierce wind was blowing the sand and snow
across an empty MSR.

'Shit!' Andrew hissed.

132

9

When a bitterly cold, wet dawn came, Andrew, Danny and Taff were laid up in shallow 'scrapes' within a circular sangar, or improvised wall, constructed from the loose rocks found about them. The sangar was positioned halfway up the slope overlooking the MSR. Protected from view by the low wall of the sangar, which blended in with its surroundings, they spent the whole miserable day watching Iraqi militiamen and reservists combing the flat plains below, obviously still looking for them. The Iraqi trucks had returned just after dawn, when the storm had abated, and were parked between two tracks of the MSR, near where Ricketts, Geordie and the others had last been seen. There was no sign of the latter and the wind-blown sand had covered up their tracks completely.

'Either they've been captured,' Andrew said,

'or they somehow managed to get off and leg out by a different route. If they don't turn up by nightfall, we'll do the same.'

'Get captured or leg out?' Taff asked, attempting some levity even though he felt as bad as he looked, which was truly dreadful.

'Leg out,' Andrew confirmed. He then looked carefully at Taff. 'Are you OK?'

'I'll survive,' Taff said.

Andrew glanced down the hill. 'I left my GPMG down there,' he said to Danny, 'when you told us to run. Even *I* couldn't carry that on the run. Now I feel naked.'

'You've still got your M16,' Danny replied, 'and that's all you'll want if we're to march all the way to the Syrian border.'

'I don't think I'll make that,' Taff said, looking serious. 'I feel nauseous and absolutely drained. Bloody awful, in fact. Why don't we try an aircrew beacon?'

'We will,' Andrew said, still glancing down the hill to the MSR, where the Iraqi troops were climbing back onto their trucks. 'They seem to have given up down there. If they have, if they leave, we'll try signalling with the beacon and hope to God that something turns up.'

At noon the Iraqis were still searching the area

below, so Andrew, Danny and Taff nibbled at the last of the high-calorie rations in their individual escape belts, checked their location with the aid of the belt's small-scale map and button compass, and decided between them what way to go when the Iraqis departed.

This they did not do until late afternoon, but finally they drove off, heading back across the MSR, the way they had come. Eventually they became no more than a puff of dust in the distant flatlands.

When the Iraqis had disappeared completely, Andrew unclipped the surface-to-air rescue beacon, or SARBE, from his kit belt. It was actually a small radio used for emergency communications between an aircraft and a party on the ground by means of a repeated, coded signal. Though they are mostly used by aircrew in case of crashes, the SAS carried them in the event of the loss of the bigger, more powerful PRC 319 radio. As they had lost that, as well as their SATCOM GPS, when they lost Ricketts and Geordie, Andrew was glad he had had the sense the bring his SARBE along instead of dumping it with his bergen. Using it, he sent a distress signal out and prayed that an AWACS aircraft would pick it up and attempt a rescue.

By sunset, this had still not happened. Ironically, just before the sun sank, an American F-15E flew overhead, but failed to see them and, as there were Iraqis in the area, sometimes along the MSR, Andrew did not dare send up a flare. The plane flew on, ignoring them.

'Damn!' Taff exclaimed hoarsely. 'There goes our last chance for today. That means at least another night in the open. I don't think I can stand it.'

'Not sitting up here, freezing our arses,' Andrew said, 'but we don't have to do that. We have to move out just to keep warm, and it's best to travel by night. When darkness falls, we should disappear.'

'I wonder what happened to Ricketts and Geordie.'

'Don't think about it,' Danny advised.

At nightfall, with Ricketts and Geordie still missing, the trio decided to push on again. After filling in their scrapes and breaking up the sangar, spreading the stones carelessly about to hide all trace of their presence, they started off and kept going until they reached high ground. This was well away from the constantly populated MSR and, with its hills and wadis, offered more protection from the elements, as well as from any Iraqis still hunting them.

Sitting on the high ground, Danny looked down through the night-sight mounted on his rifle. Scanning the flat plains, he could see for at least five miles, but there was no sign of the missing men. In the end, he decided to move on, away from the dangers of the MSR.

Still using a button compass and the small-scale map from Andrew's escape belt, they continued marching for another four hours, on a north-easterly bearing, over flat rock. By 0500 hours, just as Danny was starting to worry that they would be caught in the open when dawn broke, they came across a small tank berm with walls of soil six feet high and deep tank tracks leading away from it.

'Shelter at last,' Andrew whispered. 'We can catch some sleep here. I'll nod off like a baby. So will you, Taff.'

He was particularly concerned about Taff, who had developed a bad cough – which could, incidentally, give away their position – and was pale and visibly shaking with exhaustion. His weakness, Andrew suspected, was a by-product of the cold and damp, as well as the long march with no decent food and minimal drink.

'Yes,' Taff said, so hoarse he could hardly speak properly. 'That's all I need . . . Sleep . . . I need sleep . . . *All* of us . . . Sleep.'

'I'll keep watch,' Danny said. 'We'll take four-hour turns.'

'You and I will take turns,' Andrew corrected him, 'and let Taff rest up.'

'Fair enough,' Danny said.

Andrew and Taff lay head-to-toe in one of the ditches of the berm while Danny lay belly-down on its rim, his SLR in the firing position, his night-sight giving him an eerie blue view of the landscape in darkness.

Andrew fell asleep almost immediately, but Taff, who needed it more, was too exhausted to sleep either deeply or for long, and tossed and turned restlessly for hours, muttering under his breath. When he actually dropped off for short periods, he groaned aloud with bad dreams.

That groaning, like his coughing, could get them all in trouble, so Danny was doubly alert as he kept his long watch.

At least we're reasonably safe here, he thought.

He was wrong. When the dawn light came up, he saw an enemy position, including what looked like a hut or a box-like vehicle, with radio aerials sprouting from it, no more than 600 yards away.

Shocked, Danny slid back into the ditch and placed his hand over the groaning Taff's mouth. When Taff opened panicked eyes, Danny placed his hand on his forehead to keep his head down and was worried by how hot it was.

'Quiet, Taff!' he whispered. 'Don't say a word!'

The sound of his voice awakened Andrew, who jerked around, instantly alert, even as the fear in Taff's eyes was replaced with a dazed look. Danny removed his hand, then let the other slide away from Taff's mouth.

'There's an Iraqi position over there,' he said. 'About 600 yards. We're pinned down again.'

'Oh, no!' Andrew whispered. 'I don't believe this shit!' He rolled over onto his belly and slid up the muddy side of the ditch to gaze across the flat, frosty earth at the Iraqi position. 'Shit!' he muttered softly when he saw it. 'Jesus Christ! Can a man's luck get worse?' He rolled onto his side to look at Danny. 'We're fucked again, Baby Face. We're gonna have to stay here all day and slip out tonight.'

'Right,' Danny said.

They were indeed forced to stay all day in the ditch. Snow began to fall again. As the blizzard continued, the ditch filled with water and they

139

lay there, unable to move, soaked and frozen. There was little water left in the bottles and all their rations were gone, except for two packets of biscuits still in Danny's escape belt. Everything else – all their kit, high-calorie rations and spare heavy-duty clothes – had gone with the bergens.

By sunset, after twelve hours prostrate in icy water, they were so chilled that they had no feeling in their hands or feet, even though the former were in fur-lined leather gloves. The cold had also penetrated their joints, knees and backs, making them so crippled that when they were preparing to leave, they could scarcely pick up their weapons. They had to put their heads down through the slings, then straighten up and let the guns just dangle.

'I've never felt so fucking awful in my life,' Andrew whispered, 'but I think I can make it. What about you two?'

'I'm OK,' Danny replied. 'I'm pretty stiff, but I think I'll loosen up when we get moving. What about you, Taff?'

Taff just stared at him. He seemed not to have heard. Sitting on the edge of the ditch, he looked like a statue. The snow was still falling.

Reaching over, Danny shook him by the shoulder. 'Hey, Taff, are you OK?'

'What?'

'I said, are you OK?'

'Yes, I guess so.'

'Come on, then, let's go.'

Taff could hardly move. They had to straighten him up first and practically push him out of the ditch. When they set off, heading away from the enemy position, protected by darkness and blanketed by falling snow, he kept falling behind. And when they waited for him to catch up, he soon fell behind again. His breathing, Danny noticed, was irregular and his gaze unfocused. At one point, when he fell behind and Danny went back to fetch him, he found him sitting, slumped over, on a low, snow-covered rock, breathing painfully and holding up his hands.

'Look,' he said, 'my hands have gone black. Why should that be?'

'You're wearing black leather gloves, Taff.'

'Am I?' Taff examined the gloves on his hands with delirious eyes. 'No, I'm not,' he said. 'My hands have turned black. Don't *lie* to me, Danny.'

'Just kidding,' Danny said. He didn't know what else to say. 'They've turned black with cold,' he finally lied, feeling guilty. 'Just put them back in your pockets and they'll soon be OK again.'

'Yes,' Taff said. 'Good thinking.' Placing his gloved hands in the pockets of his jacket, he stood up again. 'You lied to me,' he said.

'Sorry, Taff.' Danny led him up to Andrew, who was shivering in the falling snow. The sergeant studied Taff, then glanced searchingly at Danny, but made no actual comment. 'Taff's hands have turned black with cold,' Danny said, deliberately and loudly, for Taff's benefit, 'and since we're looking after his weapons, I told him to put his hands in his pockets.'

'Right,' Andrew replied. 'Understood.'

'They're warmer now,' Taff informed him.

'Good,' Andrew said. 'Let's move on, men.'

They marched for another hour, but the blizzard was getting worse. Taff coughed a lot and talked to himself and kept falling behind. Aware that he was gradually losing his senses due to hypothermia, Danny tried to keep Taff's thoughts focused and his legs moving by saying how good it would be when they got back to Hereford, to the base and their comfortable bashas, to warm pubs and good bitter.

'I don't know anybody in Hereford,' Taff said, sounding annoyed. 'I come from Wales. From . . .' He tried to think of the name, failed to recall it, stopped walking to give it more thought, then started walking again. 'None of your fucking business,' he mumbled with tears in his rheumy eyes. 'Fucking cold! Who are . . .?' Suddenly, he glanced sideways, at an invisible person beside him. 'What are *you* doing here? Who asked you to come here?' The stranger did not answer and Taff looked more confused. 'What time is it? Where are we? I'm cold. Who won the Derby?'

When he didn't speak his teeth chattered, so he spoke a lot. As long as he spoke he kept walking. When he tried to think he stopped walking. His lips had turned blue, his face a ghastly yellow. Some tears had actually frozen on his cheeks and made his skin look like glass. He was coughing and shivering.

Andrew and Danny stuck with him, going back for him, dragging him on, but eventually they started suffering from cold and exhaustion themselves. Convinced that he, too, could feel hypothermia setting in, Andrew feared that they would not last the night. Yet he kept going, forcing himself to concentrate, still checking their bearings with a pocket light and button compass, determined to get as far as possible before the dawn broke again.

'Escape and evasion,' he whispered. 'Escape and evasion. That's all you've got to remember.

Keep going, boss.' He was talking to himself, but not in delirium like Taff. Instead, he was coaxing himself to go on by parroting a well-known maxim from the Combat and Survival phase of Continuation Training and recalling what that training involved – concealment, route selection, the laying of false trails, living off the land, moving carefully. It was all coming back to him. 'Always carry your escape belt,' he whispered. 'Don't despair. Never give up. Come on, boss, keep going.'

Danny, who heard every word he said, knew just why he was saying it.

By now they were on very high ground, being swept by sleet and driving snow, crossing dangerous patches of ice with bare rock between. The stars were bright, framed in patches between dark clouds, and at times they were just like the ice glinting under their frozen desert boots.

Danny stopped to gaze down at the ice. When he looked up, Taff had disappeared.

'Shit,' Danny whispered, 'I'm tired of this.'

'What?' Andrew asked, also stopping.

'Taff has fallen behind again,' Danny said.

'Go get him,' Andrew said quietly. 'We can't leave him out there.'

'I know,' Danny replied.

He made his way back, easily tracing their uncovered footsteps in the thick snow, expecting to find Taff in a minute or two, but not doing so. When he finally found him, a good twenty minutes back, he was sitting against a rock face, practically covered in snow, his eyes closed, his blue lips frozen in the grimace of death.

Danny checked carefully, ensuring that Taff was dead, and knew at once that there was no doubt about it. Brought down by hypothermia and exhaustion, Taff had finally given in.

Danny said nothing. There was nothing to say. He waited until his friend was buried completely by the snow, then he went back to join Andrew and give him the news.

Andrew just nodded, too cold to speak. Then they pressed ahead, into the swirling snow.

10

If the road-watch teams were relying on concealment as their best ally, the mobile fighting columns led by Major Hailsham, with the expert help of Sergeants Jock McGregor and Paddy Clarke, were anything but covert. Each column consisted of about a dozen four-wheel-drive vehicles – the Land Rovers dubbed Pink Panthers, and light-strike vehicles, or LSVs – plus motorcycle outriders such as the flamboyant young trooper 'Johnny Boy' Willoughby, who could fire his Browning 9mm high-power handgun with one hand while driving his Honda with the other. Though the bikers were notoriously flamboyant in word and deed, they merely summed up the general nature of Hailsham's mobile fighting columns, which were not only overt, but extremely daring and, some would say, reckless.

The columns' Pink Panthers had proven their worth in the first raids into the Scud box a few weeks before. The American LSVs, while they tended to break down too easily, were gradually becoming valued for their speed and 'invisibility' in hit-and-run raids, though certain SAS officers harboured reservations.

'I felt like Buffalo Bill,' was Jock's assessment. 'Just riding in there with all guns blazing. Fucking fantastic, boss!'

'I know you found them exciting,' Major Hailsham replied calmly. 'You thought you were in a dodgem car in a funfair in Glasgow. Fast they may be, Sergeant, and wonderful to handle, but they *do* have a terribly small fuel tank and also tend to break down.'

'Bullshit,' said Marlon 'Red' Polanski, the US Army Master-Sergeant recently attached to the SAS from 1st Special Forces Group. 'Those little babies are in a class of their own. We've only had complaints from the SAS. You guys are spoiled rotten.'

'We're British,' Hailsham said, as if that explained everything.

'What the hell does *that* mean?' Red responded. 'You need more than the rest of us?'

'Certain standards, dear boy. High expectations.

We're not into mass-produced toys produced to warm a child's heart.'

'Beg your pardon, boss?' Jock said.

'No offence meant, Jock. I merely mean that the LSV, so beloved of the Delta Force, does not necessarily excite the SAS, nor even meet all of its requirements.'

They were drinking in a tent in Wadi Tubal. Not allowed alcohol in this Muslim country, they were making do with tonic water with ice and lemon. But as this tasted like an alcoholic drink, they were all feeling high.

'Goddammit,' Red said, 'I just don't believe this garbage. You go into the goddam desert, you raid Iraqi mobile units like Indians attacking a wagon train – in out and like whirling dervishes, always highly successful – and you do it in our LSVs and *still* complain they're no good. You must be outa your mind!'

'I didn't say they were *no* good,' Hailsham replied. 'I merely said they had faults.'

'Not as good as the old Pink Panther, right?'

'Exactly, my dear Master-Sergeant.'

Polanski grinned at the grinning Jock, then looked back at Hailsham. 'Does that mean you're not using them again?'

'No, Master-Sergeant. Surely that's why you're

here. To bear witness to how we use your little toys and offer advice.'

'I guess that's right, Major.'

'So when we next go out into the desert, we'll be taking the LSVs and you, our good-natured American friend, will be coming with us.'

'Terrific,' Red said. 'So, tell me, Major, how are your road watch teams doing?'

'Not too good at all.'

'They don't have our LSVs.'

'They don't have *any* transport, Master-Sergeant, which is why they are suffering so.' Hailsham waved his hand to take in the vast, barren plains stretching out on all sides of the tents of Wadi Tubal. 'They are somewhere out there, beyond that far horizon, legging it, doing God knows what, either surviving or failing. We will know in due course.'

Red shook his fine American head in confusion or disbelief. 'Goddammit,' he said, 'you Brits are so goddam cool. I can't figure you guys.'

'There's nothing to figure,' Hailsham said. 'We merely live by a simple rule.'

'What's that?'

'Who dares wins.'

While the road-watch teams were engaged in Scud

Alley, their movements unknown, Hailsham's mobile fighting columns, after being replenished and serviced by badged SAS soldiers and REME mechanics (or REMFs – rear-echelon motherfuckers) at the Wadi Tubal rendezvous, 87 miles inside Iraq, penetrated once more into the western wilderness.

Where initially their penetration had been limited to 25 miles because of fears that Israel would respond to the battering of Tel Aviv with a full-scale invasion of the same objectives as those allocated to the SAS and the USAF, the former's successful raids against the Scud bunkers and mobile launchers had removed that threat, leaving them free to roam where they wished and pick a broader range of targets. This they could do in an area of approximately 240 square miles, including the motorway linking Baghdad with the Jordanian capital, Amman. It was a critically important military area filled with an incongruous mixture of heavily armed Iraqi soldiers on mechanized transport and impassive robed Bedouin on camels.

In addition to their normal arsenal of devastating weapons, all of the Pink Panthers now had anti-aircraft and anti-tank missile carriers with, fore and aft, protective 360-degree-traverse

Browning 0.5in-calibre machine-guns. Most of the weapons were fitted with thermal imaging sights, and the drivers, including the men on the motorcycles, wore night-vision goggles.

The Pink Panthers looked even more exotic than before as the men had since added their personally stencilled silhouettes of 'kills', including Scud launchers and communications towers, to their already colourful paintwork.

'I don't envy you guys if the Iraqis catch you,' Red Polanski informed Major Hailsham as they studied the stencilled silhouettes. 'You're practically begging to get the sons of bitches mad.'

'No offence meant,' Hailsham replied. 'They're just a few little doodles.'

'Fucking A,' Red replied. 'A few little Van Goghs. All set to be framed and hung up in Saddam Hussein's bedroom. You guys get caught with those things on your cars and you'll be in *bad* shit. You'll learn how controversial art can be when it has the wrong audience. We're not talking art criticism here – we're talking dragons and dungeons.'

'My men don't play games,' Hailsham said.

Racing across the vast, flat plains, their wheels churning up clouds of dust, the Pink Panthers and LSVs were accompanied by the bikers, with

Johnny Boy right out in front, a *shemagh* veiling his face, tinted glasses protecting his eyes and an unofficial vivid-red scarf billowing out behind him. As usual, he had an M16 strapped across his back, a Browning 9mm pistol at his hip and a leather-encased Fairburn-Sykes commando knife slipped into one of his high-topped desert boots. Together with his *shemagh*, trailing scarf, tinted glasses and blackened face, his weapons made him look bizarrely heroic.

'If that kid's as good as he looks,' Red said to Jock, who was expertly driving their Pink Panther, 'he'll be pretty impressive.'

'He is,' Jock replied. 'What about you, Master-Sergeant?'

'I'm not as young as that kid,' Red replied, 'but I do OK, I guess. Not bad for an old man.' In fact, with two tours of Vietnam, a Purple Heart, a Bronze Star, and three years of covert activity with the élite Delta Force behind him, including service in Grenada and Panama, Red was a 'soldier's soldier', and certainly looked the part – sixteen stone of solid muscle, still handsome for his age, and deeply tanned by the sun of many countries. 'You ever see that movie, *Apocalypse Now*?' he asked.

'Yeah,' Jock said, glancing distractedly at

the fleet of Pink Panthers, LSVs and Honda motorbikes racing across the desert in a long line, their wheels churning up a cloud of sand about a quarter of a mile long. 'Bloody terrific.'

'You remember that scene where the officer says with real regret, "Someday this war's gonna end"?'

'Yes, boss, I do. Robert Duvall. A great actor. Him and his yellow scarf.'

'Well, Sergeant, that's what I've felt every day of this war. Someday – in this case, very soon – this war's gonna end ... and I'm gonna regret it. That's a terrible truth.'

'It's the nature of the beast,' Jock replied. 'That's why we're all here.'

As the mobile columns made their way across the desert, the men going without lunch as morning became afternoon, RAF reconnaissance GR-1A Tornadoes from the airfield at Tabuk, in the far north-west, flew constantly overhead, heading for Baghdad, where they would use radar techniques to drop 1000lb bombs from 20,000 feet with pinpoint accuracy. Also seen frequently were heavily armed F-15s, F-16 Fighting Falcons, A-10s and A-6E Intruders on round-the-clock patrols – both north, where the Delta Force were operating, and south, where the SAS columns were heading.

Throughout their long journey to the location chosen for their laager, or fortified position, the men in the columns came in contact with no enemy transports or tanks, though they did see more than one caravan of Bedouin, in fluttering robes and astride camels burdened with carpets and bags filled with wares. The Bedouin watched the extraordinary columns of Pink Panthers, LSVs and motorbikes with interest, but did not seem unduly surprised.

'They have their own, unique lives to lead,' Hailsham explained to his driver, Paddy, 'and probably think we're as insubstantial as the wind – here today, gone tomorrow. When we're gone, the desert will still be here – and so will the Bedouin.'

'I feel weird when I see them,' Paddy replied. 'As if I'm living a history book.'

'I know what you mean, Sergeant.' Hailsham waved his hand to take in the other Pink Panthers, LSVs and motorbikes spread out across the desert, roaring and churning up great clouds of sand as they made tracks through the flat plain. 'Here we are in our armoured transport, with all these technological marvels, and there they are travelling by camel as if time has stood still. That's what makes it seem strange.'

The columns kept going, as if racing one another, not stopping for food or rest, to reach their destination before sunset. That destination was merely a convenient gathering place, a base, an Empty Quarter to be used as a jumping-off point for their many patrols outward in all directions.

Once there, in their Empty Quarter, a small holding force made a base, then the various groups broke up and went off in different directions to form a series of OPs and laagers across a broad front, though close enough to be able to reach one another other if help was required.

By last light, Hailsham's group had formed themselves into a half-squadron laager – a temporary fortified position of Pink Panthers and LSVs in the shape of a wagon-wheel – and were settling down for the night, with some men taking turns to sleep and stand guard.

By sunrise, though the main laager was still in position as a temporary, camouflaged base camp, the various Pink Panther and LSV crews were taking turns at prowling about the open expanse of flat, stony desert between Karbala, south-east of Baghdad, and Nukhaib, about sixty miles from the Saudi border.

There was no cover in this area. It was mostly flat, sandy desert with little sun and too much wind, appreciated only by the frequently seen Bedouin. The Iraqi militia were not spotted so often, though they certainly crossed the desert roads in soft-topped trucks and tanks. For this reason, Hailsham's men made a point of peering into culverts under main roads to check whether they concealed Scuds or other mobile units. If that happened to be the case, they took the Iraqi troops out with a withering hail of unexpected gunfire, then destroyed the Scuds or mobile big guns with plastic explosives or, failing that, with their trusty sledgehammers.

Passing Bedouin often witnessed them doing this, but showed no sign of curiosity, let alone outrage.

The ways in which the SAS men waged their mobile desert war were many and diverse. They blew up passing enemy trucks with their M19s, which could hurl small but potent 40mm armour-piercing grenades more than a thousand metres. They also blew up bridges and communications towers with a variety of explosives, including TNT, Semtex and C3/C4 plastic explosive. They illuminated entry points to enemy targets with large, tripod-mounted designators to enable the laser-guided GBU-15 and Paveway II bombs of the Allied aircraft to hit home with devastating accuracy.

Often dressed as Arabs and speaking Arabic, sometimes even riding camels, they moved dangerously close to enemy bases and establishments, even infiltrating their towns and villages, to bring back important information on armaments factories, oil refineries, communications and transportation systems, radar sites and command and control centres. This information was relayed via the SATCOM equipment on their backpacks to HQ in Riyadh, which passed it on to the AWACS aircraft on the prowl for fresh targets.

'Without us,' Paddy said, 'those fucking pilots wouldn't know shite from shinola. We're their eyes and their ears.'

'I'm sure they appreciate that,' Major Hailsham replied distractedly, gazing across the vast expanse of the desert and wondering where his missing road-watch team was.

'I hope so,' Paddy said. 'Fucking pilots!'

Even more dangerously, the SAS patrols would drive close to enemy airstrips, camouflage the

Pink Panthers, LSVs and motorbikes, go the rest of the distance by foot, locate the supply dumps, usually located near the edge of the base, and contaminate the aircraft fuel under the very noses of the Iraqi guards.

Johnny Boy often did this by himself – in unusual ways.

'I drive around the airstrip on my Honda,' the trooper informed US Master-Sergeant Red Polanski, whom he admired and was admired by, 'in full view of the Iraqi shitheads on guard. I'm wearing my *shemagh* and my face is painted brown, so when I wave like I'm just having fun, they think I'm a local nut. I do this until last light, when the lazy shits are half asleep, then I circle around to where the supply dumps are located and get off the bike. If no one's there, I go in – just cut the barbed wire with shears – and go about doing what I have to do. That's all there is to it.'

'And if someone's there?' Red asked, always keen to know every detail.

'I have a good piss in the sand, unconcerned, just another A-rab, and when the guard turns away, which he often does in disgust, I slip up behind him with my neat commando knife, slit his brown throat and enter via the gate as if I

own the joint. I then contaminate their petrol –
sorry, Red, their gasoline – and walk out and
dawdle back here on my Honda.'

'Hold on!' said Red, always looking for a weak
spot. 'If the fuckers find a dead guard by the tanks
they're gonna know something's up.'

'Too true,' Johnny Boy replied, enjoying the
challenge, thrilled to win. 'And for that very
reason, when I have to silence a guard . . .'

'A typical Brit euphemism for something
really nasty,' Red interrupted. 'I love it, kid.
It's so cool!'

'When I have to silence a guard,' Johnny Boy
continued, 'which will let them know it's sabo-
tage, I deliberately tape an explosive charge to the
petrol tanks. When they find it, they think they've
been smart and know what I was up to. They
remove the explosive charge and never think to
examine their fucking petrol. Thus, for the next
month or two, they have nothing but trouble with
their aircraft, tanks and troop trucks – which is
more valuable to us than simply blowing up the
supplies. A good job well done, right?'

'Right,' Red replied admiringly.

Apart from their ambushes and acts of sabo-
tage, the SAS men collected intelligence on enemy
command and control centres, bunkers, and

nuclear, chemical, and biological weapons, as well as troop and aircraft movements. They also snatched enemy soldiers and either interrogated them or handed them over to the green slime, the Intelligence Corps to be given a hard time.

Sometimes, when specifically asked to find a prisoner for urgent interrogation, they would be compelled to take considerable chances. One method was to make a daring attack on a passing truck or column by racing up in their speedy light-strike vehicles, firing and throwing grenades while on the move, then hauling a surprised soldier into the LSV and roaring off in a protective cloud of sand caused by the explosions. Another was to sneak up on an enemy camp under cover of darkness and simply abduct one of the guards, silencing the other guards, if necessary, by slitting their throats.

These approaches, however, only produced prisoners of lowly rank, most of whom could impart little information. For more valuable prisoners they had to be more daring, which sometimes involved high-risk raids into the heart of passing convoys. In such raids, SAS troopers would hurl grenades and fire their small arms as the Pink Panther carrying them raced boldly between selected Iraqi vehicles to cut out the one containing officers. While the other Pink Panthers formed a buffer between the first Land Rover and the Iraqi column, SAS troopers in an LSV, often led by Red Polanski, would speed alongside the isolated officers' vehicle, shoot all of its occupants except one, abduct the survivor at gunpoint and then race away to safety, protected by the guns and grenades of the other Pink Panthers and LSVs. The latter would then also make their escape, using the smoke dischargers on the rear of their vehicles to create a protective screen behind them.

'I've got to hand it to you Brits,' Red Polanski said admiringly, 'you sure as hell know how to shake out. I've never seen anything like these goddam raids – and I've seen a lot. That kid on the motorbike, those guys in the Pink Panthers – dammit, even myself in the LSVs – like red Indians attacking a stagecoach in a Hollywood movie. Who said the British were inhibited? Not out here, they aren't!'

'You're too kind,' Major Hailsham said.

'Don't tell me it was nothing.'

'It was nothing,' Major Hailsham said. 'We're just doing our job.'

'Stop being so goddam humble. I hate Brit

humility. What you guys are doing in this desert is unprecedented. You're way out on your own, man.'

'I'm sure the men would be pleased to hear that.'

'So I'll tell 'em.'

'Please don't. The SAS encourages humility as well as humour, so I don't want you swelling their heads. Your Delta Force might need its ego stroked, but the SAS doesn't.'

'That's a crock of shit, Major.'

'It's a fact of life, Master-Sergeant.'

'Jesus, you guys are so cool you make sweat look like ice cubes.'

'Rather nice in the gin and tonic.'

'Which we can't drink in this damn country. Tell me, Major, have you had any news from your missing road-watch team?'

'Alas, no,' Hailsham said.

Increasingly, as the war continued and the Coalition forces advanced, Hailsham's men were coming across many Iraqi wounded abandoned by their comrades in battle, plus deserters only too glad to be captured. The finding of 'quality' prisoners for interrogation was therefore becoming a lot easier. In fact, over the first few weeks such Iraqis became an embarrassment, even a liability, to the SAS, as they required food, first aid, a place to stay and generally looking after.

'A bullet in the head and a grave in the sand,' Paddy suggested as a practical means of solving the problem. 'It's what they'd do to us.'

'Damn right,' said Red.

'Wrong,' Hailsham informed him. 'We can neither break the Geneva Convention nor give the Arabs of either side an excuse to call us imperialist barbarians. We must therefore treat all our prisoners with respect, consideration and kindness.'

'British pragmatism at its best,' Red commented with a wicked grin. 'There's even a sound reason for your so-called moderation. It sure as hell ain't straight from the heart.'

'Hearts are easily broken,' Hailsham said, 'and we can't afford breakage. More tea, Master-Sergeant?'

Often the individual Pink Panther and LSV teams would stay away from their temporary base, or laager, for more than a night or day, in which case they would construct their own camouflaged lying-up position, or LUP, and use it for sleep or short-term breaks. At such times Hailsham would luxuriate in the silence, in the grandeur of the desert sky, and recall earlier SAS tasks, which some, more romantically inclined, might describe as adventures.

In particular, he recalled the Falklands war, when he had first come to know his then revered superior, Major Parkinson, now with the Queen's Regiment, Sergeant-Major Ricketts, then a sergeant, and all the others now missing on that road watch.

Major Hailsham, then a captain, had been renowned for his sardonic tongue, but now, though his tongue remained acerbic, he was filled with concern.

There had been no radio call from the road watch team. No SARBE beacon. No communication via SATCOM. Helicopters sent over the area had found no trace of them. They had literally vanished. Now, even running his own successful campaign in the desert, Major Hailsham could not help but worry. Where the hell were they?

The night before Hailsham's columns were due to regroup and drive back to the Wadi Tubal rendezvous for resupply and debriefing, four Iraqi artillerymen, attempting to avoid a strike by a US A-10, drove off the road and across the desert – straight into the sentry position of Hailsham's half-squadron laager.

Without thinking twice, the SAS troopers

keeping watch in the semicircle of Pink Panthers poured Browning machine-gun fire into
the oncoming vehicle, killing three of the Iraqis,
one of whom virtually somersaulted out of the
car and thumped onto the desert floor. The
survivor, shaking visibly, climbed down with
his hands raised and was instantly escorted to
Major Hailsham, who spoke fluent Arabic.

Questioning the frightened young soldier,
Hailsham learnt that he was the commander
of his gun battery and a mine of information about the activities of the Iraqis in
the area. The value of his intelligence was
greatly increased when the prisoner produced
the military maps that his men had been carrying. These described, to a trained eye, the
detailed deployment of all the enemy brigades
in western Iraq.

Realizing immediately that his work here was
finished, Hailsham relayed the information back
to the Tactical Air Coordination Centre, then
ordered his men to destroy their LUPs, break
up the laager, hide all evidence of their stay
in this place and prepare to drive back to
Wadi Tubal.

Even as they were leaving, heading into the
setting sun, Allied bombers were striking the

positions marked on the Iraqis maps and relayed to the TACC by Major Hailsham.

Had it not been for his missing road-watch team, Hailsham would have been pleased.

11

Andrew and Danny walked all night. Just before dawn they came off the high ground, down a slight gradient, and ended up in a shallow wadi, only three feet deep. There they lay, cuddled together for warmth. Normally in such circumstances they would have been hot-bedding, or sharing a sleeping bag between them, but since those had gone with the bergens, they just lay close together for the warmth that would prevent hypothermia.

As SAS troopers never discussed the dead, or those who 'beat the clock', neither said anything about Taff's death, though both were deeply grieved by it.

'Real cosy,' Andrew said, trying to lighten their load a little.

'Shut up,' Danny replied. 'I don't need your jokes.'

'Gee whiz, you're so sexy.'

'Shut up!'

'I's just all in a dizzy, little darlin', to have you so close.'

'One more word and I'm moving away from here.

'My lips are sealed tight.'

Andrew chuckled, but said no more after that. In truth he was too cold, his teeth practically chattering. If he, a fleshy man, felt that way, he knew that Danny felt worse.

It was a long, miserable night and Andrew hardly slept. He was now too exhausted to sleep properly, which only made matters worse. His thoughts were slipping and sliding, shifting in and out of gear. One minute he was thinking of his wife and children back in London, the next he was wondering how the hell to get out of this mess.

They still had rifles and hand-grenades, but everything else was gone. Even the high-calorie rations in their escape belts were finished and now they were starving. Left in the escape belts were the small-scale map and button compass, pocket knife, fishing line and hooks, hexamine fuel blocks and matches, but they were unlikely to catch any fish here, nor any other kind of food that could be gutted and cooked over a fire.

In fact here, in this freezing, wind-blown desert terrain, they dared not even light a fire, for fear that the smoke would give away their presence to the Iraqis. So they were in bad shape, gradually freezing, slowly starving, and if a miracle did not occur tomorrow they would be in worse trouble.

Unable to sleep, Andrew turned to look at Danny and realized that although he was nearly thirty, he still looked like a kid. He was rightly called 'Baby Face', and had the shyness to match, yet he also had the instincts of a killer and scared the hell out of everyone.

Danny had always baffled Andrew. He was like the late Hollywood actor Audie Murphy. Before becoming a film star, Audie Murphy had been the most decorated GI of World War Two, having killed an extraordinary number of German soldiers. Yet he was every bit as shy as his baby face made him seem. Always wanting to be a soldier, Andrew, when a schoolboy, had been particularly impressed by Audie Murphy playing himself in a film about his war years. In that movie, *To Hell and Back*, Murphy had looked like a kid and killed like a machine.

Danny had always impressed Andrew for the same reason. He was a baby-faced, shy, killing machine who rarely made a mistake. All his mistakes, as Ricketts had pointed out, were in his personal life.

This got Andrew thinking about Ricketts and the others. Where the hell were they? Had they managed to escape from the MSR? And if so, where had they gone and what were they doing? Indeed, were they even still alive?

Big Andrew shuddered at the thought that they might have been captured by the Iraqis. The green slime had confirmed that activities against the Scuds had badly frightened the Iraqis and made them embark on a determined hunt for SAS troops. If they caught any they would not treat them kindly – and the Iraqis, as Kuwait had taught the world, were quick to use torture.

That possibility lodged in Andrew's exhausted thoughts and took wildly exaggerated, haunting shapes, making him even less inclined to surrender to sleep.

He did, however, drop off for short periods, but his feverish thoughts and the constantly howling wind did not permit much sleep. Mercifully, the sky cleared and the sun rose in a clear blue sky that was not exactly hot, but warm enough to begin drying their sodden clothes and thawing their frozen limbs.

Looking around him, Andrew saw only the wadi, more rocky, hilly, frosty terrain on all sides, and a brooding, cloud-filled sky. Though the snow had stopped falling, the wind was still harsh and moaning like the voices of the damned.

'What do we do now?' Danny asked.

'We keep going,' Andrew replied. 'The march will warm us up. Also, we've got to find food and drink. But first I'm going to check my damn feet. They both hurt like hell.'

While a slightly refreshed Danny kept watch, Andrew pulled off his wet desert boots with great difficulty to find that his feet were swollen and badly blistered.

'Shit,' he said, 'this isn't going to help me.' He tried wrapping them in bandages from his kit belt, but his feet were so swollen that he could not get them back into the boots with the bandages on. Setting the bandages aside, he removed the small knife and matches from his escape belt, sterilized the knife by holding it in the flame of a match, then gritted his teeth and proceeded to lance the blisters one by one. It took quite a bit of time and hurt like the devil. It hurt even more when he swabbed the raw wounds with TCP. Thinking at one point that he was going to faint from pain, he nevertheless managed to complete the job. He then smeared two separate short strips of bandage with antiseptic cream, placed them once around his feet, providing only one extra, thin layer, and managed by so doing to get his soaked, filthy desert boots back on. His heart was racing from fighting the pain, but it was fading now.

Rolling around until he was lying on his belly beside Danny, he took hold of his SLR and gazed to the front. An Arab appeared at the bottom of the wadi with a big herd of goats.

'Damn!' Danny murmured, sliding his M16 into the firing position and flipping the sight up.

'Hold on,' Andrew cautioned him, placing his big hand on Danny's frail wrist. 'What are you doing?'

'I'm going to take that bastard out,' Danny said.

'Why?'

'Because he's coming right towards us, you bloody fool, and he'll soon be on top of us.'

'So what? He's just a goatherd.'

'An *Iraqi* goatherd,' Danny corrected him.

'He's a civilian,' Andrew insisted. 'You can't shoot a civilian.'

'Just watch me,' Danny said, taking aim along the sight and sliding his itchy finger to the trigger.

'He's a Bedu,' Andrew tried. 'The Bedouin are reported to be friendly to our cause, so he might actually help us.'

'I'm taking no chances.'

'He could help us,' Andrew said.

'He could turn us in,' Danny replied.

'Why the fuck would he care about that? He's not a soldier – he tends goats – and if we offer him some of our gold, he's not likely to say no. That gold would be a fortune to a guy like him.'

'Sorry, Andrew – no way.' Danny was still aiming along the sight, but now sliding his finger over the trigger.

'Look,' Andrew said more desperately, squeezing Danny's wrist, slyly trying to coax his finger off the trigger, 'he's a Bedu, which could mean he's friendly. He's also poor, which could mean he's greedy. Let's wave the gold under his nose and see what he says. He gets the gold if he takes us to the border. Come on, Danny, let's try it.'

By now, the goatherd, wearing a turban, an ancient coat of dark tweed, a long, tattered scarf and a pair of thongs, was sitting on a rock and idly watching his flock milling about at the end of the wadi.

Danny studied him through the sight, then slowly, reluctantly, withdrew his itchy finger from the trigger. 'Just go and ask him where we are,' he said. 'No more than that. I don't trust the bastard.'

'Sure,' Andrew said. 'Right.' Leaving his SLR on the ground, he stood up, waved his hand in a friendly manner and called out a greeting in Arabic. Surprised, the old goatherd looked up, but otherwise made no move. Still speaking fluent Arabic, which he had been taught at the Hereford and Army School of Languages, Andrew told the goatherd not to worry, explained who he was, and asked if he could come and talk to him. Not moving from where he was sitting, the man nodded agreement.

After glancing down at Danny and indicating with a wave of his hand that he should do nothing for the moment, Andrew walked along the wadi to speak to the goatherd. When he reached him, he saw that he was very old, with a thin, weather-beaten, good-humoured face. After exchanging a formal greeting, Andrew asked the old man if he spoke English.

'No,' the old man said in Arabic. 'I'm sorry.'

'It's me who should apologize,' Andrew replied, speaking the same language, 'because my Arabic is so poor.'

'It is a pleasure to find a foreigner who speaks it at all,' the goatherd said. 'What are you doing here?'

Andrew explained the situation, then asked the old man if they were far from the Syrian border.

'No,' the Arab said, shaking his head and pointing north-west. 'It is not very far. About ten kilometres in that direction.'

'Can you take us there?'

The Arab shook his head again. 'I am sorry,' he said, 'but I cannot afford to lose my goats. They are my sole livelihood.'

From his kit belt Andrew produced the pouch containing approximately £800 in small gold pieces, as well as the chit stating in Arabic that Her Majesty's Government would pay the sum of £5000 to anyone returning the bearer to friendly territory. He handed the old man the chit, waited until he had read it, then took hold of the Arab's wrist, turned his hand over and poured some gold pieces into it.

'You can have the rest,' he said, 'when you

deliver me and my friend to friendly people over the border. Will you do it?'

Smiling, the old Arab dropped the gold pieces, one by one, into the side pocket of his tweed coat. Then he stood up and nodded. 'Yes,' he said. 'Go, fetch your friend.'

Andrew returned to Danny and said, 'Hand me that SLR, mate. We're on our way home.'

Sitting upright, Danny passed the SLR to Andrew. 'No, thanks,' he said.

'What?'

'I'm not going,' Danny said.

'What the fuck do you mean, you're not going? This old guy is going to take us to the border. He's friendly *and* greedy.'

'If you believe him, go with him,' Danny said, 'but I'm not going with you.'

'For fuck's sake, Danny, he's OK!'

'I'm not trusting any Arab,' Danny said, 'and I don't think you should.'

'OK,' Andrew said. 'You believe what you want, but I'm going with him. Besides, the Iraqi search parties are closing in and we double our chances of evasion by splitting up.'

'We also reduce each other's odds on individual survival,' Danny replied. 'Bear that in mind, Sergeant.'

'I could order you to come for your own good,' Andrew said.

'You could, but you won't. That's not the way we do things.'

'Shit, Danny . . .'

'It's OK, Andrew, you go. I'd just rather not join you.'

'Too bad,' Andrew said.

'Your choice, Sarge. Have a safe trip.'

'Same to you, mate.' Andrew nodded, grinned, then went to join the goatherd, who was already walking away from his animals and clambering out of the wadi. Andrew glanced back at Danny, who looked frail and terribly alone. As if sensing Andrew's unhappiness, Danny suddenly waved and called out to him. Andrew stopped. 'What?'

'If anything happens to me and you survive, write a poem about me.'

'I will, mate, I promise. It'll be there in the Imperial War Museum for your children to read.'

'Right. Good luck, Sarge.'

'Same to you, Trooper.' Instantly feeling a lot better, Andrew waved again, then turned away and followed the Arab out of the wadi.

'How long did you say it was?' he asked when they had walked for five minutes.

'About ten kilometres,' the Arab replied. 'It will not take too long.'

In fact, it took less time than Andrew had anticipated. They walked for about twenty minutes, crossing some more rocky terrain with low hills on either side and a wedge-shaped stretch of desert in the distance, muddy brown in weak sunlight. Andrew checked his button compass, making sure they were heading north-west, and when he saw that they were he relaxed and looked up again.

At that moment, the Arab fled – surprisingly fast for an old man – shouting out that the man behind him was a British soldier.

Directly ahead of the Arab was a laager of soft-topped trucks, mobile anti-aircraft gun units, and heavily armed Iraqi militiamen, all staring at Andrew.

'Shit!' Andrew exclaimed, shocked, betrayed, momentarily frozen.

Regaining his senses, he turned and ran the other way, heading for the protection of the rocky outcroppings nearby. He heard shouting in Arabic, followed by firing rifles, and glanced over his shoulder to see the soldiers aiming at him, even as bullets kicked up dirt around him and ricocheted off the stones.

The militiamen ran towards Andrew and he stopped to return their fire. He managed to get off a short burst before he was hit. 'Shit!' he cried out again – the one word he could think of – then he felt his leg bursting with pain and giving way beneath him. He kept firing as he fell, his bullets whining into the sky, then collapsed onto hard stone and dust as the Iraqis surrounded him.

Excited, almost hysterical, they kicked him repeatedly, bent down and punched him, hammered him with their rifle butts, then grabbed him by the shoulders and hair and brutally hauled him across sharp, cutting stones to the vehicles of their laager.

When they dragged him between two trucks, into their camp, his real suffering began.

12

Major Hailsham and his men approached the elaborately camouflaged fixed missile site at night, guided to it by Trooper Willoughby. Parking the Pink Panthers and LSVs a good half mile away, they completed most of the journey by foot, then dropped to the ground and crawled on their bellies the final hundred metres or so, eventually taking up positions in a depression in the desert floor, forming a front a quarter of a mile long, just south of the site.

Hailsham studied the target through binoculars, using night-vision goggles. This missile site was the real thing, not an expensively built decoy. In the cold blue light of the goggles, he saw a missile-launching area, adjoining command posts, guidance systems, two separate radar areas, supply dumps and early-warning stations with automated sensors on high observation towers – all behind steel fences covered in barbed wire and patrolled by armed guards.

Right now, as he could clearly see from the activity in front of a concrete bunker and command post, a salvo of Scuds were being prepared for a multiple launch, possibly aimed at Israel. According to Intelligence, Saddam Hussein was still hoping to draw Israel into the war with another, unexpected Scud attack from a fixed missile site within range of that country. The green slime had therefore obtained the approximate location of the site and ordered Hailsham to find the exact location and take out the site. Now here he was with most of his squadron, lying belly-down in a useful hollow in the desert floor, looking up at a sky containing a full moon and brilliant stars. There was no wind tonight.

'I don't think we can take it ourselves,' he said.

'Neither do I,' said US Master-Sergeant Red Polanksi, likewise lying belly-down in the sand close to Hailsham. 'It's too widespread. There are too many troops. We wouldn't get in and out in time.'

'Let's blow a few fences, boss,' Johnny Boy

said from the other side of Hailsham. 'Take a few down with the MILAN and then race in and back out in the dinkies.'

'You're just spoiling for a fight,' Paddy Clarke said. 'This is all the Boy Scouts to you.'

'The Boy Scouts are from your day,' Johnny Boy retorted. 'They're not part of my background. So what do you say, boss?'

Hailsham shook his head. 'I say no. As our American friend noted, it's too widespread, there are too many troops and we'd never get in and out in time.'

'I'd be in and out like a whirling dervish,' the reckless trooper said, 'throwing grenades left and right.'

'Grenades wouldn't be enough,' Paddy objected. 'Even the MILAN wouldn't do it. We need heavier fire-power, but we wouldn't have the time to set it up. There's too much to be taken out in there and it's spread far and wide.'

'Correct,' Red said. 'What we need is air support. We'll have to call in a US strike force.'

'I thought you'd say that,' Hailsham said.

Red grinned. 'Sure. Why not? We need to flatten that goddam place – and for that we need really heavy air power within reach of this area. I suggest you let me call up a flight of the latest

F-15Es, or Strike Eagles, of the 336th Tactical Fighter Squadron.'

'What's so special about them?' asked Johnny Boy, always keen to learn from his older, more experienced, American hero.

'They're special all right,' Red answered, equally keen to advise his admirable, and admiring, young British protégé. 'Single-seat, 1600mph motherfuckers designed to attack ground targets using the Lantirn system.'

'The *what*?'

'Lantirn – with an "i". Low altitude navigation and targeting infrared for night. It's carried in two pods – one for navigation, the other for laser-targeting – both linked to the pilot's electronic helmet visor, which magnifies the target fifteenfold.'

'Sounds like Star Wars stuff,' Johnny Boy said, clearly intrigued.

'It is, kid. Short of firing laser beams as weapons, the Lantirn system is the ultimate in Star Wars technology, achieving better than ninety per cent accuracy and capable of dropping bombs within ten metres of the target on the first pass.' He turned to Hailsham. 'Believe me, Major, you couldn't do better.'

Hailsham thought about it for a moment.

Putting the binoculars back to his eyes, he studied the target once more. Removing the binoculars and night-vision goggles, he rubbed his tired eyes.

'What about the automatic early-warning sensors on those observation towers?'

Red sighed. 'The Strike Eagles'll be preceded by an EA-6B Prowler. Its avionic system includes five pods containing jamming transmitters. They fire streams of radio waves and electrons on seven different frequencies. The Prowler's wingtips pick up the target's radar waves and feed them into a computer that gives the frequency info needed for the jamming. One Prowler's enough to jam all the radars on that missile site. Once they're jammed, we can pinpoint the targets with our laser pistols.' When Johnny Boy whistled with admiration, Red grinned triumphantly. 'Should I get on the SATCOM?'

'The wonders of science,' Hailsham said. 'Yes, get on the SATCOM.'

As Red was relaying his request and grid references back to Saudi Arabia via the SATCOM system in the charge of Paddy Clarke, Hailsham crawled along his line of widely spaced men, stopping at the ones with portable laser designators to tell them which targets he wanted pinpointed once the Prowler had passed over and jammed the enemy radar. On the way back he stopped to have a few words with the men on the GPMGs and mortars, telling them not to use them unless fired at. By the time he returned to Master-Sergeant Polanski, the American had finished his transmission and was holding his thumb up.

'They'll be here in no time at all, Major. Just sit back and relax.'

'Thank you for the suggestion, Master-Sergeant. I might just do that.'

Reaching his original position, Hailsham rolled onto his stomach and again examined the missile site through his binoculars. In the eerie blue glow of his night-vision goggles, he saw that the Scuds, just recently wheeled out of the hangars on their mobile platforms, were being raised to an elevation suitable for long-range firing. Many armed guards and engineers were gathering around them.

'I think we got here just in time,' he said to Red. 'It looks like they plan to launch those things later tonight, or perhaps tomorrow at dawn. Another surprise attack.'

'More of a surprise,' Red said, 'since the Israelis think the Scud attacks have ended. Wouldn't *they* get a shock!'

'Let's hope they won't,' Hailsham said.

'You can depend on the good old US of A. Those planes will be here in no time.'

'I live by faith,' Hailsham said.

Red rolled over and grinned at Johnny Boy, who was lying on his back with his hands behind his head and his long legs crossed. The kid was only 24 and looked as cocky as they come, but as Red had already found out, he had nerves of steel, initiative and a lot of guts. Red liked the Brits generally, but Johnny Boy really amused him. He was like Red had been when he first joined the Marines – bright, straightforward, easily bored, in desperate need of adventure and excitement, willing to take chances for it. When he looked at the trooper, Red was looking deep in the mirror.

'Hey, kid,' he said.

'Yes, Red, what is it?'

'How long have you been in the Army?'

'You mean the Regiment? The SAS?'

'No, I mean the Army – in total.'

'Three years in the Army – one with the SAS.'

'What made you join?'

'Come on, Red, you know that. What the fuck made *you* join?'

Red laughed and slapped the kid's shoulder.

'Kid,' he said, 'you got no respect. That's court-martial language. But you're right, we both know why. Fun and games, right?'

'That sums it up, Red.'

'Some soldiers have better motives, kid.'

'Each to his own, Red.'

'You been in Belfast or Antrim?'

'Both,' Johnny Boy replied. 'Don't tell me you disapprove, Red. I hate American Irishmen.'

'What did you do over there, kid?'

'Not much that I enjoyed. I didn't have a motorbike then, and it rained all the time. Also, it was full of people like Sergeant Clarke, if you know what I mean.'

'Hey, knock it off!' Paddy said.

'Sorry, Sarge,' the trooper replied. 'I thought all Irishmen had wax in their unwashed ears and that you wouldn't hear me.'

'I heard you all right. It's hard to ignore someone farting. One more verbal fart like that and your handsome mug'll look like a pomegranate. That's blood-red, for your info.'

'Hear you loud and clear, Sergeant.'

'Stop interrupting,' Red said to Paddy. 'I'm trying to talk to the kid, here. Where do you come from, Johnny Boy? I mean, where were you born and raised?'

'England.'

'I *know* that, kid! Where?'

'The only place worth living in that country.'

'You mean London?'

'Right. Crouch End. That's in North London, Red. It's near Finsbury Park, where a lot of Sambos and Paddies have their beds, but I didn't mind that.'

'Johnny Boy!' Paddy exclaimed.

'Sorry, Paddy,' Johnny Boy said. 'A mere slip of the tongue in the night. I need my sleep, don't you know.'

'Are you working-class, kid?' asked the American.

'Sergeant *Clarke* is working-class . . .'

'Fuck you, Trooper!'

'. . . but I'm middle-class, English, and proud of it. My dad's an interior decorator . . .'

'He means a painter and decorator,' Paddy clarified helpfully.

'. . . and my mother runs the wallpaper shop and does my Dad's accounts. They're pretty decent, my parents.'

'So why did you join the Army?' Red asked, always eager for facts.

'Because my home life, though decent, was

fart-boring and I couldn't find work. So here I am, Red.'

'You're a good kid,' Red said, thinking of his own kids back at home and feeling a little emotional. 'You're a bit on the wild side, I reckon, but otherwise you're OK.'

'Thanks, Red, so are you. Not bad for a Yank.'

'Read you loud and clear, kid.'

The bullshit continued for another thirty minutes or so until it was interrupted by Major Hailsham, who quietly said, 'There's the plane.'

The Prowler was high overhead, its lights shining like two stars, its grey underside laden with five pods that made it look like a great pregnant bird. It came no lower, not needing to risk low altitude, but it flew directly over the missile site, then turned around to come back again. Hailsham picked up his binoculars and studied the missile site. The guards in the observation towers were pointing up at the Prowler. Yet they were unconcerned. It was too high up for an attack plane. The guards watched it as it circled back over the site and then returned to where it had come from. When they saw that it was definitely leaving, they relaxed again.

'Is that it?' Hailsham asked.

Red was back on the SATCOM, just finishing his transmission. He faced Hailsham and stuck his thumb up in the air. 'That's it,' he said. 'The Iraqi radar is jammed. The Strike Eagles were flying in just behind it and are practically here. Start painting your targets.'

Johnny Boy removed his hands from behind his head, uncrossed his long legs, sat up and turned to the front. 'I've got to see this,' he said.

Using the PRC 319, Hailsham contacted the groups with the portable laser designators and told them to illuminate their selected targets for the incoming aircraft. Within minutes the various designators had 'warmed' or 'painted' their targets with a spot of intense light that could be picked up by the aircraft and would enable their missiles and bombs to be directed to the targets with incredible accuracy.

The flight of Strike Eagles arrived within minutes and came in low and fast, looking less fat-bellied than the Prowler, but more terrifying, with high twin fins, F100-PW-220 turbofan Pratt & Whitney jets, and a payload of AIM-9L Sidewinders, AIM-74 Sparrows and M61A1 20mm rotary cannons. Sweeping down and across the desert with awesome precision, one after the other, creating a godalmighty roar, they released two missiles at a time, raked the site with their cannons, levelled out and were ascending even before their missiles had struck home. Hitting their targets with shocking violence, the missiles made the ground erupt, spewing earth, sand and smoke, the latter streaked with yellow flames, and blowing the buildings apart with a cataclysmic, deafening fury.

The command posts were blown apart, the great radar bowls buckled, the supply dumps burst into flames, and the observation towers, also torn apart by the cannons, eventually collapsed, with men hurtling down, screaming, through the falling debris. Other men suffered worse, set ablaze and burning alive, running to and fro like balls of fire while their world exploded around them.

The Strike Eagles flew away, practically disappeared, returned, came back down with missiles searing and cannons thundering, then shot away again. The steel fences melted. Another building went up in flames. More burning men were screaming in the smoke that billowed up, black as oil, like heavy curtains, to meet the cascading sand. The Strike Eagles made a final run, getting rid of their payloads, and the devastation, as spectacular as it was hideous, was finally complete.

When the Strike Eagles saluted and flew away, back to base, the once widely spread, heavily guarded missile complex had been reduced to a grim pile of blazing, smoking rubble piled up around a few skeletal buildings, smouldering corpses and some shocked, dazed survivors.

'Let's bug out,' Hailsham said. He stood up and used hand signals to notify the other men. The hand signals were passed along the long line and the men started moving out.

A great mushroom cloud of exploded sand and smoke was spreading over the blazing, smouldering ruins of the missile site as Hailsham gratefully turned his back to it.

'Impressive, right?' Red asked with a broad, boyish grin.

'Oh, yes,' Major Hailsham said.

'Brilliant!' Johnny Boy exclaimed excitedly. 'Like a fucking great light show. Knocked 'em for six, Red!'

'We hit it right on the nose, kid.'

The stench of scorched flesh and burning fuel was being carried on the breeze as the squadron legged it back across the desert floor to the vehicles parked half a mile away. Hailsham stood up in his Pink Panther, beside his driver, Paddy Clarke, about to give the hand signal, when a column of sand obscuring the stars to the west drew his attention.

'What . . .?'

'Fucking Iraqis!' Johnny Boy exclaimed as his Honda motorbike roared into life. 'Let's get the hell out of here.'

Hailsham dropped his hand, clearly illuminated in the moonlight, as Paddy switched on the ignition and revved up the engine. The other vehicles did the same, one driver hearing the other, then they all raced away from the missile site with a discordant roaring.

The wheels of their vehicles churned up more sand, advertising their whereabouts.

Johnny Boy cut away from the column and headed directly towards the advancing Iraqi trucks.

Red looked on in disbelief as the LSV he was in, driven by an SAS Trooper, raced on ahead.

'What the fuck's he doing?' he asked the driver.

'Just causing some aggro,' the driver said, not fazed in the slightest.

Johnny Boy roared straight at the advancing Iraqi trucks on his motorbike, his headlamp turned off, and unholstered his Browning with one hand while holding the handlebars with the other.

193

He kept racing towards the column, hardly noticed in the darkness, and then turned sharp right, cutting across the oncoming trucks, and emptied his 13 rounds into the lights and windscreens he passed. Some of the lights went out. He heard glass shattering. One of the trucks careered sideways and crashed into another as Johnny Boy turned left, letting the Iraqi trucks pass him, and circled to come back up their rear.

Holstering his hand gun, he unclipped a phosphorus grenade. He let go of the handlebars, unpinned the grenade before the handlebars started shaking, then grabbed them again with his free hand and lobbed the grenade straight into the rear of the truck in front of him.

He again turned sharply to the right and was roaring away, out of range, when the grenade exploded in the back of the truck, in the very laps of the troops, blowing the canvas covering off and causing jagged fingers of white flame and streams of phosphorus fireflies to fan out through the darkness as the flying canvas burst into flames and fell smoking to earth.

The truck veered sideways and, as the first had done, smashed into another one.

Johnny Boy was already racing back to his own column when the Iraqis in the remaining trucks opened fire with their small arms. The bullets, which were not aimed at him, as he was well out to the side and still practically invisible, whistled dangerously close to him as he turned in and headed back to his mates.

'Nice one, Johnny!' he whispered.

Hailsham saw the colliding trucks, the grenade explosion and burning canvas, but also saw that the other trucks were still in pursuit. Not wanting a long chase, as this limited the use of fire-power, he used hand signals, which were passed from one vehicle to another, to tell the men to form the Pink Panthers and LSVs into a circular laager. They did so and then unwrapped their arsenal of GPMGs, MILANs, Stingers, 60mm LAWs, 81mm mortars and small arms just as Johnny Boy came roaring out of the moonlit plain and skidded to a halt between Major Hailsham and US Master-Sergeant Polanski.

The trooper swung his leg off the motorbike, propped it up on its support, unslung his M16 from his shoulder and went to join Red, who was crouched down behind his LSV, about to take aim with his own M16.

'I caused a bit of confusion out there,' Johnny Boy said, trying not to sound too proud.

'It's a pity you didn't stop 'em,' Red said. 'Here they come, kid.'

The Iraqi trucks, all lights blazing, came out of an immense cloud of sand created by their own wheels. They stopped within rifle range, disgorging their troops, just as Hailsham dropped his right hand and the SAS opened fire. The GPMGs roared relentlessly as the MILANs, Stingers, LAWs and mortars backblasted, sending their bombs raining down on the Iraqi trucks with devastating results. More shooting flames and boiling smoke. At least two trucks exploded. The Iraqi troops ran left and right, escaping the explosions, spreading out to return the fire, as the SAS opened up with their small arms and caused more devastation. More Iraqis screamed and fell, but the others remained courageous, spreading out and setting up their own mortars in the midst of that withering fire. Their mortars spewed flame and smoke and then the first shells exploded.

Hailsham was deafened, then covered in showering sand. When his ears cleared and his vision returned, he looked up from where he lay and saw a blackened shell hole in the ground just in front of Red's LSV, positioned beside Hailsham's Pink Panther. Red and Johnny

Boy were OK, still behind the LSV, but the front of the vehicle had been badly damaged and its tyres had burst into flames. Sand was raining down everywhere. Dense smoke obscured the view. Hailsham clambered back to his feet, saw his damaged SLR, unholstered his Browning and walked up to Red. The American and the young trooper were firing their M16s. Hailsham was about to say something – he didn't know quite what – when a wave of nausea assailed him and he had to sit down again.

'Are you OK, boss?' Paddy asked. 'That exploding mortar shell knocked you for six.'

'A little dizzy,' Hailsham said. 'What's happening, Paddy?'

'We've held them back, boss, but they're a stubborn bunch of bastards. They're digging in there. We've knocked out all their trucks and taken out a lot of men, but the ones left aren't going to let us go. You've got to admire them, boss.'

'This is no time for admiration, Paddy. Do you think we can hold here?'

'Well . . .'

'No,' Red said, crawling up on his hands and knees, though with his M16 held in one hand and his lips grimly set. 'We may have knocked out their trucks and downed a lot of their men, but one of those left still has a radio and is using it right now. You know what that means, Major? More Iraqi troops nearby. I say we shoot and scoot, Major, before the others get here. We won't stand a prayer otherwise.'

'OK, gentlemen, let's go.'

Hailsham's head had cleared and he stood up again. 'Relay the message to everyone,' he said to Paddy. 'Tell them we're bugging out. Tell them not to wait for further orders – they're to take off right now. They all know where the FOB is and they've got to get back under their own steam. OK, let's get to it.'

Paddy rushed around the laager, passing on Hailsham's message, as Hailsham clambered into his Pink Panther, smacking an ear to clear it, even as more Iraqi mortar shells exploded nearby.

'What about me?' Red said, ducking as exploding sand spewed over him. 'My LSV's in the wrecker's yard.'

'Come with me,' Johnny Boy offered. 'On the back of my bike. Have yourself an adventure.'

Red glanced at Hailsham.

'Why not?' Hailsham said. 'Most of the Pink Panthers, including mine, are full up – and Willoughby's reliable.'

'Hi, ho!' Red said. He climbed up on the motorbike behind Johnny Boy, just as Paddy returned from the far side of the laager. Paddy took the driving seat of the Pink Panther and looked directly at Hailsham.

'Yes, boss?'

'Yes,' Hailsham said.

Paddy put his foot down and the Pink Panther roared into life, shooting out from the circular laager and cutting a track through the sand. The other vehicles did the same, breaking away one by one, following Hailsham across the flat plain, away from the Iraqis. As the latter had no working trucks left, since most were in flames, they could only offer a fusillade of small-arms fire that did little damage.

One final Iraqi mortar shell, however, fired by the bloody fingers of a wounded militiaman, looped down to the rear of the Pink Panthers and LSVs that were making their escape across the desert. It exploded just as Johnny Boy was roaring past on his motorbike with Red Polanski sitting on the back, a great smile on his sunburnt face.

The explosion lifted the bike up in the air and flipped it into a spin that sent Johnny Boy and the American in opposite directions before they crashed down again.

Hailsham didn't know they were gone until it was too late.

'We can't turn back now,' he said when he realized they were missing. 'Let's just pray that they make it.'

13

Ricketts made it. When the Iraqi trucks advanced across the dark MSR, with the militiamen fanning out between them and firing on the march, he, Geordie and the other three troopers, Gillett, Moorcock and Stone, were saved by the curtain of swirling sand and smoke created by the phosphorus grenades. Down on one knee, in the firing position, with Geordie beside him and the troopers spread out behind them, returning the fire of the Iraqis, Ricketts saw the headlights of the advancing trucks blink out, shattered by bullets, as the smoke and sand from the explosions of the phosphorus grenades formed a spectacular curtain that temporarily obscured the view for both sides.

'Let's shoot and scoot,' he said to Geordie, 'while those bastards can't see us.'

'Right,' Geordie said. 'Got ya.'

'We head south along this MSR for about five hundred metres, but spreading out at different angles, then turn left and head straight for those hills behind us, spreading out again to hit the bottom of the hills at five different locations. When we get approximately three hundred metres up the hill, we'll all move in the direction required to meet the others. It's not exactly a precise rendezvous, but it's all I can offer. OK?'

'OK, boss.' Geordie turned back and relayed this information to the other three, even as they continued pouring fire into the smokescreen separating them from the advancing Iraqis. Each man stopped firing just long enough for Geordie to impart his message. 'Right, boss,' each trooper said in turn, then started firing again. When the last man had confirmed he understood, Geordie nodded at Ricketts.

'Shoot and scoot!' Ricketts bawled, rising to his feet and firing from the hip. '*Shoot and scoot*!'

In an SOP, or standard operating procedure, originally designed for jungle warfare, the five men immediately made a tactical withdrawal that involved splitting up and taking different routes to their emergency rendezvous while returning a heavy barrage of fire for as long as possible, thus confusing the enemy, who would think the fire was coming from all directions. In this case, they were aided immeasurably by the curtain of falling sand and swirling smoke, which must have made their separate, relentless bursts of gunfire appear to the Iraqis lost in the sand and smoke to be coming from more men than there were.

For Ricketts and the others the tactic worked, confusing the Iraqis long enough to let them race southward along the MSR, protected by the billowing smoke and sand, firing as they ran, before turning back and heading straight for the hills where, Ricketts knew, Andrew, Danny and Taff had already gone.

Briefly parted from the others as they all took different routes toward the hills, Ricketts reached the lower slopes just as the smoke was clearing from the MSR and some Iraqi troops, bolder than the others, raced in his direction.

Ricketts dropped to one knee, resting his M16 on the ground, and pulled a grenade from his ammo belt as he jumped up again. It was another phosphorus grenade, designed to do maximum damage, but even before it had completed its downward arc, he had followed it with a smoke grenade.

The grenades went off one after the other, even

as Ricketts was picking up his M16 and hurrying up the lower slopes of the frosted hills. The first explosion was spectacular, erupting between the Iraqi troops, blowing some into the air, and tearing the darkness with fingers of silvery light and showering phosphorus fireflies. The second exploded a second later, less spectacular but just as effective, creating a choking smokescreen that completely blinded those not wounded or killed by the first. By the time the smoke cleared, exposing the dead and wounded to the other Iraqis, Ricketts was well up the lower slopes of the hill and out of their sight.

They gave up the chase after that. Ricketts saw them from the hill. They were milling about on the smoky MSR, checking their dead and wounded. As Ricketts, smiling, started backtracking to meet up with the others, the Iraqis were picking up their casualties and putting them in the trucks. By the time Ricketts had reached Geordie and his three troopers, the Iraqi trucks were driving away, back across the MSR, gradually becoming lost in the cloud of dust churned up by their wheels.

'They haven't forgotten us,' Ricketts said when he met up with the Geordie and his men, all having made it safely to the hill. 'They have our location and they'll probably send choppers or planes. We better move out immediately.'

'What about Andrew, Danny and Taff?'

'No one saw them on the way here?'

The other three shook their heads.

'Then we have to forget them. We can't comb these hills for them. Either they made it or they didn't. If they did, they should be well on their way by now, striking out on their own.'

Ricketts looked at the other three men, the recently badged probationers, and asked, 'What about you men? Are you OK?'

'Sure, boss,' Trooper Stone, always the coolest of the three, said with a wide, cocky grin.

'I'm fine, too,' Gillett said. 'I had a few moments back there on the MSR, but I think I'm OK now.'

'Moorcock?'

'No problems.'

'Are you sure?'

'I think so. I mean, I'm feeling pretty tired and sometimes a bit confused, but I guess one is caused by the other . . .'

'It is.'

'. . . and apart from that, I think I can make it.'

'Were you frightened back there?'

Moorcock looked a little embarrassed. 'Well . . . yes, I was frightened. Why not admit it? Yes, boss, I was.'

'Good,' Ricketts said. 'That means you're not dead yet. What about you two back there? Were you frightened as well? Don't be scared to admit it.'

'Not me,' Stone said. 'I swear to God, I wasn't frightened. Maybe a little bit *nervous*, but not actually frightened.'

'Being nervous helps,' Ricketts said. 'What about you, Gillett?'

'I thought I was shitting my trousers, but I managed to hold it in.'

'Your probationary period's over,' Ricketts said. 'You men have all earned your winged badge. OK, let's march.'

The first day was long and arduous, with snow and sleet dogging the group, as well as search helicopters sent over the MSRs by the few Iraqis who had survived the previous battle. It was early morning by the time they crossed the low hills, but by the late afternoon, having to lie low repeatedly to let the choppers fly over, they had only covered about three miles.

The night was better, bringing some respite

from the search parties, and they managed to cover another twelve miles or so before first light. Unable to build a proper LUP, since the required equipment had been discarded, they rested in scrapes until noon, then struck out again.

There were fewer helicopters by then, but there were more ground troops, not only combing the area for them, but also on the look out for the troops of the élite Delta Force, the American equivalent of the SAS, who were known to be working inside Iraq's second main Scud reserve – the northern Scud box, known as Scud Boulevard, located along the border with Syria.

'That's where we're going,' Ricketts explained, checking his small-scale map and button compass. 'To a place called Al Qaim, near the Syrian border. We should find friendly forces there.'

They were relatively lucky for most of the journey, making good progress over three nights and two days, but the nearer they came to the northern Scud box, the more populated was the area, with the many intersecting roads, long used for trading between the locals and those across the frontier, becoming increasingly busy. Ignoring the war going on in their midst, the locals, dressed in the traditional *keffia* and *dish-disha*, carrying their wares on makeshift rucksacks on their backs, on rickety old carts hauled by donkeys, or on camels, often with vicious dogs snapping around them, went about their unchanging business as if all was normal.

In this area the Iraqis, fearful of attack from the northern Scud box or invasion from the border, were particularly nervous and opened fire on anyone not instantly recognizable as a local trader. Ricketts and his men were therefore not surprised to often find dead civilians on the roads and in the fields, or by the banks of the Euphrates river, their corpses torn to shreds by the local wild life and covered with bloated, frantic flies.

'Cor, what a pong!' Geordie said, holding his nose as they passed one such corpse. Geordie was in file behind Ricketts, but temporarily caught up with him by hurrying to get away from the stench. 'Those fucking Iraqis should get rid of these poor buggers, not just leave 'em as food for wild dogs and flies. Just leavin' 'em could cause an epidemic worse than fucking AIDS.'

'You've had AIDS, Geordie?'

'Don't come it, Sergeant-Major. You get that fucking disease, you don't survive it, from what I've been told.'

'From experienced friends, right?'

'No, Ricketts – wrong. There's no bleedin'

poofters in *my* circle, so don't try it on. I just read about it in the papers, is all. I've come no closer to the fucking disease than that, so don't suggest otherwise.'

'Just a thought,' Ricketts said. He was just amusing himself, passing the time, trying to find some distraction from the pain of his blistered feet, his exhaustion, his hunger and his thirst, during this last leg of the journey to Al Qaim. The remaining high-calorie food in their escape belts was gone, the water had gone even sooner, and now they were all beginning to suffer from the lack of replenishment. Thank God, they would reach the border town in a matter of hours.

'Let's take a break,' he said. It was nearing last light and he wanted to make the final leg of the journey by night. Relieved, the men settled down in a semicircle, Ricketts and Geordie sitting together, and the three troopers lying on their backs to stretch their legs and rest up.

'Tell me, Ricketts,' Geordie said, 'what did you do before you joined the Army?'

'I was a toolpusher – first on the North Sea oil rigs, then in the oilfields in the Gulf.

'So you know this area already!'

'Not *this* area,' Ricketts said, 'but I knew Kuwait as it was about fifteen years ago.'

'You had a good time?'

'I had my wife and kids with me, which certainly helped a lot, but you couldn't do any boozing and there wasn't too much else to keep you busy. I was glad to get home.'

'What do you think of the A-rabs?'

'I respect them. They can be volatile and cruel, but they're also proud, good-humoured and generous. We could learn a lot from them.'

'You joined the Army when you returned from the Gulf?'

'More or less. I got a job as a salesman for the oil company, couldn't stand it, became pretty bored with middle-class life and decided I'd rather fight in Belfast than sleep soundly at night. I joined up, served my time in Northern Ireland, then applied for the SAS. I've never regretted it.'

'Yeah, everyone knows you love it, Ricketts. So what will you do when this show's over and they give you a desk job? I mean, at your age they're not likely to let you go on active service again.'

'No, they won't. I think this is the last time.' Ricketts shrugged, expressing regret and resignation. 'I don't think I could stand a desk job – not even with the Regiment – so I guess I'll take early retirement and sign on with a security firm. Even that would be better than pushing a pen.'

'You could become a mercenary.'

'I don't approve of them.'

'Then become a military instructor for Third World countries. They're always looking for experienced former soldiers and anyone with your track record would be a gift to them.'

'That's a thought,' Ricketts said. 'But I think I'm at an age where my wife's going to expect me home a bit more, so I'll probably end up as a security guard.'

'You could do worse,' Geordie said.

Ricketts glanced over his shoulder and saw that the sun was sinking, casting last light on the horizon and, he hoped, on the border. 'OK, men,' he said. 'Let's strike out again.'

Wearily, the men climbed to their feet and fell without thinking into file formation, with Geordie out front on point, troopers Gillett, Moorcock and Stone in the middle, and Ricketts bringing up the rear. They progressed without incident for another two hours, then stopped for another break and to let Ricketts check his small-scale map with the aid of a pencil torch.

'According to this map,' he said with a deep surge of pleasurable anticipation, 'we're only six miles from Al Qaim. I therefore suggest that we get up and go before what energy we have left deserts us. If we stay here too long we'll become too lethargic to move. So let's move right now and get it over with.'

'I'll second that,' Geordie said.

When the three troopers agreed, all keen to get to safety, they climbed to their feet, picked up their weapons, and started across the dark field, away from the Euphrates, toward the lights shining from what they hoped were friendly houses in the distance.

They had only been walking five minutes when the first shots rang out.

'*Shake out!*' Ricketts bawled and they all threw themselves to the ground as bullets whipped over their heads to ricochet off the rocks behind them. They were returning the enemy fire from a belly-down position even before they actually saw the Iraqi troops approaching from the front, spreading out, silhouetted by the lights around Al Qaim, firing on the move.

There were a lot of them, Ricketts noticed, as he fired his SLR. Far too many to be dealt with. The only way forward was to go back and circle around. Ricketts stopped firing and waved his right hand to draw the attention of the

others, all of whom were firing their M16s and
SLRs at the mass of shadowy figures zigzagging
towards them.

'We meet between those palm trees,' Ricketts
shouted above the shocking din. 'Right there by
the river. OK? *Shoot and scoot!*'

They all jumped to their feet and ran sideways,
towards the river, spreading out and firing their
weapons on the move. Some Iraqis fell, but the
others kept moving, shouting warnings to one
another as they fired.

Trooper Moorcock was ahead of Ricketts,
zigzagging like the Iraqis, firing on the move,
but then he suddenly jerked back, his beret flying
off his head, followed by pieces of splintered bone
from the back of his skull as his weapon sailed
out of his upraised hands and he crashed onto his
back. He was already dead when Ricketts leaned
over him to check, so Ricketts jumped up and
continued running, holding his SLR against his
waist and firing on the run.

He heard the sound of a mortar firing and
tried to shout a warning. The shell exploded
between Geordie and Stone before he could do
so. Geordie managed to keep running, but Stone
was less lucky, being picked up by the blast and
turned over and slammed down again.

He had been crossing the field diagonally, heading away from Ricketts, intending to confuse the Iraqis as part of the SOP of shoot and scoot, so now he was too far away for Ricketts to help him. However, as Ricketts kept running, he saw Stone standing up again, holding onto his wounded elbow and limping towards Gillett, who was rushing over to give him covering fire. Unable to walk – clearly wounded in the foot or leg as well as in his elbow – Stone collapsed again. Gillett was standing between him and the Iraqis, keeping up a protective hail of gunfire with his M16, as Ricketts plunged into the shade of the palm trees by the river-bank.

Looking back, he saw Gillett dropping his gun and raising his hands above his head. The Iraqis surrounded him, forced him onto his belly, aimed their weapons at him and Stone, but did not fire at them. Instead, a few stood guard while the others spread out again and advanced towards the river, this time not firing.

'*Ricketts*!'

Looking along the river-bank, Ricketts saw Geordie hurrying towards him, at the crouch and still holding his SLR. When he reached Ricketts, he straightened up and stared across the dark, moonlit field at the advancing Iraqis.

214

'They're obviously well-disciplined militia-men,' he said, 'so Gillett and Stone might be OK. What the hell do *we* do?'

Ricketts studied the advancing Iraqis, then stared over the river. The water was icy, about 400 yards wide, flooding the banks and flowing quickly.

'The only escape route left is north,' he said. 'That means crossing the river.'

'Are you fucking joking?' Geordie asked. 'That river's in flood. The current's too strong. It'll sweep us away.'

'We have to take that chance, Geordie. Either we do that or we stay here. Do we toss or decide?'

Geordie studied the river with growing trepidation. 'Did you ever see that movie, *Butch Cassidy and the Sundance Kid*?'

'Yes,' Ricketts replied.

'Who's Butch and who's Sundance?' Geordie asked.

'Let's find out,' Ricketts said.

After hurriedly discarding their weapons, kit belt and desert boots, they walked to the flooded bank and tentatively dipped their toes in to check the temperature and strength of the current. The water was ice-cold and the current was fierce.

They gazed at one another, momentarily unde-
cided, then glanced back over their shoulders to
see that the Iraqis were still advancing and would
soon be at the line of palm trees, practically on
top of them.

'Fuck it,' Geordie said. Then he took a deep
breath and plunged in, followed by Ricketts.

The shock of the icy water took Ricketts's
breath away and momentarily blotted out all
thought. It was even colder than he'd expected,
already numbing much of his body, and he
realized that if he was in it too long, he'd
freeze to death before he reached the far bank.
That bank was far away and the current was
very strong, having already swept Geordie off
course and now doing to same to Ricketts, no
matter how hard he struggled to swim against it.
Nevertheless, he kept going, no longer having a
choice, and was spurred to greater efforts when
gunshots rang out and the water spurted up near
him where many bullets were striking it.

Ricketts went under and stayed down as
long as possible, though the total darkness,
fiercely tugging current and lack of feeling in
his chilled limbs was disorienting and filled
him with the fear that he was making no
progress at all, or might even be swimming

towards the bottom rather than across to the far side.

Though normally possessing nerves of steel, he experienced a fleeting panic of the kind he had not known since childhood. It made him burst through the surface, where he soon saw that he was in another area, well away from the palm trees where the Iraqis had been firing, and out in the middle of the river.

Geordie, he noticed when his eyes had cleared of water, was still swimming as well, though much slower, now slightly behind, and a good way upstream.

Ricketts kept swimming, fighting against the fierce current, making headway, but with agonizing slowness, being swept along even as he managed to inch forward, closer to the far bank. Now he felt numb all over, except for darting pains in his feet, and was scarcely able to move his hands when he dipped them in the water.

His lungs were on fire. He was breathing in spasms. The river roared and splashed, pummelled him and froze him, but he fought vigorously against it, swimming, always swimming, and at last reached the far bank.

Scrambling halfway out, Ricketts was swept sideways and almost fell, but hurled himself forward again, hitting the bank with a soft thud and sinking into the mud. Rolling over and kicking himself backwards, he kept going until all of him was free of the rushing water. Relieved, he rolled over onto his belly, retching and gasping for breath for some time.

When eventually he looked up, he saw Geordie a lot further along the bank, also lying face down, but barely moving. Though dripping wet and shivering with cold, Ricketts clambered to his feet, almost toppled over with dizziness, recovered and made his way carefully along the muddy, slippery bank to where Geordie was lying, wet and covered with mud. Ricketts shook him gently by the shoulder, calling his name.

Geordie rolled over. He was breathing with shocking harshness and stared up with dazed eyes.

'Did we make it?'

'Yes, Geordie, we made it.'

'I'm not sure that I did.' He tried to sit up but failed, hardly getting his shoulders off the ground, so Ricketts knelt beside him and helped him into a sitting position. 'Fuck,' Geordie gasped, 'I feel awful. I can hardly breathe. My heart's racing. I can't feel a thing.'

'You'll be OK in a minute or two, Geordie. Just take your time.'

Geordie just nodded, trying to control his raucous breathing, shivering even more than Ricketts had done, as if out of control. Looking along the bank, Ricketts saw a ruined mud hut just beyond it, surrounded by a few scraggy palm trees, illuminated by moonlight.

'That house looks uninhabited,' Ricketts said. 'Let me help you over there. At least we'll be out of this wind and can stay there until we dry out. Do you think you can make it?'

'With your help,' Geordie gasped.

Ricketts slipped an arm around Geordie's back, sliding it up under his armpits to give him leverage. Even with such assistance, Geordie could hardly stand and Ricketts had to practically carry him all the way, from the rushing river and fierce, freezing wind to the relative shelter of the palm trees around the mud hut. The hut was falling down and had only half a roof, but the walls would offer protection from the wind. Ricketts helped Geordie inside. The floor was covered with rubble and rubbish, but at least it was dry. Ricketts managed to clear a space of sharp-edged debris and laid Geordie down.

'OK?'

Geordie nodded, though he looked and sounded awful. His face was a ghastly, deathly white and his breathing was anguished. His lips and hands had turned blue.

'We're only a mile or two from the border,' Ricketts told him. 'I think we've made it, Geordie.'

Geordie closed his eyes and tried to catch his breath. 'Cold,' he managed to croak eventually. 'Can't feel anything . . . Hurting, too . . . where it's not cold . . . Need to be warm.'

'I know,' Ricketts said, 'but we can't light a fire. If we do, the smoke will give us away. We'll just have to dry out.'

'Not dry,' Geordie murmured. 'Wet and cold . . . Feeling sick and . . .' He choked and then coughed up more water and what looked like blood. 'Fuck you, Andrew, I'm OK.'

'I'm not Andrew,' Ricketts informed him, suddenly realizing that Geordie was very ill. 'I'm Ricketts – Sergeant-Major Ricketts. Try to stay awake, Geordie.'

'Sleep . . . Good idea . . . Need sleep to wake up . . . You keep watch, Baby Face . . .' He coughed again and spat more blood. 'Mum? Is that you, Dad? Why's it so dark in here? I won't do it. *I won't*!'

He soon started rambling, becoming inco-
herent, the words spilling out in a torrent of
recollection and hallucination. He was icy to
the touch, obviously dying from hypothermia,
and eventually, as Ricketts had feared, he sank
into a coma.

Ricketts didn't have a thing to cover him up
with when he went to find help. The man he left
lying in that rubble was a shivering wreck.

Across the rocky field, looking away from
the river, Ricketts saw the lights of another
dwelling. After hurrying across to it, through the
striations of dawn's pale light, he peered through
the window and saw that it was inhabited by
an Arab family. The children were still sleeping,
while their parents were squatting on woven mats
on the floor and eating what looked like boiled
rice or couscous from an earthenware bowl. An
older man, wearing traditional dress, was seated
in a chair near the wall, reading a book by the
light of a flickering oil lamp. Forced to take a
chance, Ricketts hurried back to the front of the
house and knocked on the door. It was opened
by the older man, who looked at him with dull
curiosity, but no sign of fear.

Speaking crude Arabic, Ricketts explained who
he was and that he had a sick man in the nearby

mud hut. 'We just want to cross the border,' he said, 'but we need some kind of transport, for which we can pay well. Will you help us?'

The old man glanced over his shoulder, obviously focusing on the mud hut, then nodded and said, as best Ricketts could understand: 'My neighbour has a truck you can hire. He lives a few hundred metres away. You go back and look after your friend while I fetch the truck.'

'My friend is very cold,' Ricketts told him. 'Can you lend me a blanket?'

The old man nodded, disappeared inside, then stepped out again, holding a thick blanket. 'Here,' he said. 'Now go. I will soon return with the truck.'

When Ricketts thanked him, he turned away and hurried along the mud track that led to the next house, visible through the early-morning mist, about 500 yards further on. Ricketts stepped off the track and hurried back across the field, towards the river, until he came to the broken-down hut.

When Ricketts hurried inside with the blanket, he found that Geordie had died. Shocked and grieving, he knelt beside his friend. After closing his eyes, he covered him up with the blanket. He then sat in the rubble, drained by an awful numbness, staring blindly at a patch of cloudy-grey sky that was framed by the hole of broken bricks in the opposite wall.

Ricketts sat there for a long time, exhausted, almost broken, until the sound of the approaching truck jerked him out of his reverie. After glancing down at the blanket, as if expecting to find Geordie alive, he stood up and went to the broken wall and looked across the rocky field.

It was not a farmer's truck that he saw.

It was a truck filled with heavily armed Iraqi troops.

'Bastard!' he exploded, then turned away, hurried across the room, glanced one last time at his dead friend, and clambered over the broken wall at the back, out of the hut.

Ricketts ran for it, bullets whistled past his head. Reaching a hill, he dropped low and rolled down it as more bullets whipped through the air above him and whined into the empty sky.

He picked himself up and kept running, heading for Syria.

14

Danny Porter struck out on his own, determined
not to be captured. When he heard the sounds
of shooting from a long way beyond the wadi,
shortly after Andrew had left with the Arab goatherd, he knew that Andrew had been betrayed
and was now either dead or in captivity. He also
knew that the Iraqis would suspect the presence
of other British troopers and intensify the search
for them. Since those British troopers came down
to one man, himself, he had no doubts that he
was in for a hard time.

Leaving the wadi, Danny walked on a pre-
arranged bearing, due north, aiming for the
Euphrates. It was thirty-six hours since he had
drunk and he badly needed water, but only
fifteen minutes after leaving the wadi, he saw
an Iraqi troop truck behind him, heading for
the spot where he had lain up. Realizing that

the Arab goatherd had informed the Iraqis of his presence, he started walking even faster, trying to forget his hunger and thirst, forcing himself to keep moving.

Alone now and feeling it, he walked for the rest of that day and night, his third on the run. Iraqi search helicopters often flew overhead, repeatedly forcing him to lie low. He had to do the same to avoid passing army trucks, all filled with troops and bristling with weapons.

Next day the sky was clear and the snow had stopped falling, which made Danny's march a little easier. But Iraqi helicopters were still searching the area and many bands of heavily armed militiamen were assiduously combing the windswept hills and valleys for him. Put off by the sight of them, he constructed a simple lying-up position and laid up for the rest of that day, only breaking the LUP down, erasing all traces of his presence, and moving on again, when last light had come.

After another nine-hour march, in the early hours of the morning, he saw the Euphrates through his night-sight. It was in a flat plain below him, a winding strip of muddy water, with palms trees and houses scattered along its banks. He also saw a small village surrounded by irrigated fields and more scattered palm trees.

As dogs were barking from the houses, he made his way down to the river's edge with great caution. Stepping into the water, he sank to his waist in soft mud and had to drag himself out. After lying belly-down to get his breath back, he sat up again and filled his water bottles.

Soaked and muddy, he laid up for the day in a dry wadi system close to the village. His morale was at a low ebb, but he remembered the disciplines of Continuation Training and managed to perk himself up a little. Though filthy, the water was drinkable and helped to quench his thirst. He finished the last of the biscuits taken from his escape belt, then tried to prepare himself for what he knew would be severe hunger pangs.

However, Danny's feet were in a bad way. He had lost most of his toenails and his blisters were suppurating. As the blisters were on the soles of his feet, they made walking an agonizing endurance test. With his adrenalin still running strongly, he did not feel particularly tired. In any case, when he tried to sleep, the air was so cold that every ten minutes or so he woke up shuddering violently.

Still in darkness, he moved off again, following the murky Euphrates, from which he was able to obtain enough water to survive. Also, by staying in the valley he avoided exposure to the pitiless windchill that had killed Taff Burgess and threatened him and Andrew with hypothermia. He was, however, in a populated area, thus running a greater risk of discovery. He minimized this by avoiding all human habitation.

Again, Danny tried to summon assistance with his SARBE rescue beacon, but without success. Probably, he reasoned, it was not precise enough to enable the SAS search helicopters to locate him. As he also knew full well, the intense Iraqi activity in the area and the widespread AA gun batteries raised the odds against a successful pick-up.

In fact, throughout his lengthy, arduous march Danny was constantly seeing Iraqi troops on the move or civilians walking about in large groups, obviously as organized search parties. To make matters worse, they were out mostly during the night when, as the Iraqis knew, he would be travelling. Because of this, he advanced at a snail's pace, being forced to repeatedly stop, scan the area through his night-sight, stop again, backtrack, watch, wait, and eventually move on, treading with care.

It made demands on his patience. He endured it either by focusing intently on his SAS training or by thinking about other things, notably home. Though taking confidence and pride from being an SAS soldier, and from his capacity for survival, Danny had always lacked such virtues in his personal life and now knew that he had been more than naïve in falling for the first girl who had showed an interest in him and letting vanity blind him to the fact that they lived in separate worlds. His wife Darlene was attractive, but she liked a good time, and now, even though they had two children, she was fooling around a lot. Danny knew this was true because his mates had told him so and his father and mother, always keen to support him, had confirmed the depressing fact.

While able to make a soldier's 'kill' as casually as slicing bread, Danny, who sliced throats instead of loaves, was otherwise too sentimental for his own good. He could not, therefore, bear the thought that his children – like him, born and bred in Kingswinford, in the West Midlands – were being brought up by a mother who liked a lively night life and spent more time away from home than in it. He knew this because his parents had told him so and were, reportedly, spending more nights with the children than Darlene could count or even remember.

'We're too old for this,' Danny's father had

complained in a phone call to the Paludrine Club in Hereford. 'So you better come home and sort her out. She's a right boozy tart, that one.'

Danny hadn't sorted her out because he didn't know how to start. He just wanted to be with the Regiment, sorting out any enemy they cared to give him, which he knew he could do well.

Now, filling time, fighting isolation and silence, embarked on a long march that could mean life or death, he reflected long and hard on his domestic problems, but decided that such thoughts were negative and possibly dangerous. He would focus, instead, on staying alive and getting home in one piece.

In the early hours of the fifth day he found another LUP, this time on a cliff face over 600 feet high. From there he could look out over the river to an Arab village located on the far bank, where the people were walking about peacefully and life seemed to be normal. For most of the day he watched men fishing in the river, pains in his stomach, saliva in his throat, constantly, obsessively thinking of how hungry he was. By last light he was practically starving and glad to move on.

That night he found himself between the river and a motorway, in a corridor which varied in width from one mile to six. As the wadi systems coming down towards the river demanded continual descents and climbs, he tried to save energy by keeping out of them and instead walking parallel with the road, which he knew was dangerous.

Indeed, shortly after taking to the side of the road, he heard the drone of a vehicle coming up behind him. Dropping immediately to the ground and looking back through his night-sight, he saw a black dot on the motorway, growing bigger each second. When it passed him, he was surprised to see that it was one of the increasingly rare mobile Scuds, its missile on the back of a noisy wheeled platform, its green tarpaulin flapping. Still not forgetting his rigorous training, Danny dutifully made a note of the time and place.

To his despair, however, he was informed by a nearby motorway sign that he was 50 kilometres further from the border than he had anticipated. This meant that he had at least one more full day and two nights on the march.

After marching for another hour, when last light was approaching, the only place he could find to 'basha down' was a rubbish-strewn culvert passing under the motorway embankment.

Six feet high and nearly ten wide, it was relatively safe, reasonably dry and protected him against the night's cold wind.

Early the next morning, soon after daybreak, he heard the jingle of bells – a familiar sound by now – as a herd of goats was ushered through the tunnel on its way to pasture.

'Shit!' he whispered, then hurried out of the culvert to hide in a nearby ditch, where he remained until the man and his goats had passed.

Knowing that the goatherd would eventually return, Danny crawled along a wadi, going to ground each time a car came down the road. Most of the cars were military troop trucks or jeeps, though some were battered old heaps driven by local workers and a few were chauffeur-driven Mercedes filled with wealthy Arabs.

After crawling along the wadi for about six miles, tearing his army trousers and cutting his hands and knees, which left a trail of blood behind him, Danny found a hole in the ground and lay there for the rest of the day. Yet another miserable day.

Moving out again that night, he found that the terrain consisted of small hills covered with scrubby thorn bushes and complex wadi systems that made him feel he was scrambling up and down through endless quarries. Exhausting though this was, dehydration was becoming a more serious problem. This was not helped by the fact that he had to keep away from the river, where most of the houses had vicious dogs whose noisy barking would give away his presence.

Finally reaching the end of the series of wadis, he headed due west and had an easier time until stopped by the barbed-wire fence of a heavily guarded military establishment.

Suddenly, an air-raid siren wailed. Thinking he had been seen, Danny immediately went to ground and searched the darkness ahead with his night-sight. He saw a number of AA gun positions, with tall towers that looked like radio masts on the high ground behind them. A surprising number of armed patrols were walking about, with a lot of the men scanning the sky as the siren continued its demented wailing.

Realizing that he had stumbled on a highly sensitive Iraqi signals command post about to be attacked by Allied aircraft, Danny stood up and hurried away, running at the crouch, weaving left and right, and praying to God that the facility was not being protected by minefields.

It was impossible to check this as the ground was in darkness and the air raid had already begun, with French Jaguars dropping their bombs from high in the night sky, well out of range of the pounding Iraqi guns. The explosions were catastrophic, shaking the ground beneath his feet, illuminating the darkness with rapidly flickering, silvery light and filling the air with crimson sparks and phosphorus fireflies.

Danny dropped to the ground, letting the shock waves pass away, then jumped out and started running again. He repeated this process over and over again until, after what seemed like an eternity, the air raid ended and the Jaguars disappeared.

Looking back, Danny saw that the main facility was now much further behind him, with many of its buildings on fire, some of the fencing blown away, other parts scorched and buckled, and a pall of smoke covering all. Nevertheless, as he now realized, that fenced-in area was only one part of the facility and the rest of it was scattered far and wide, over a broad expanse of land filled with wadis and ditches, criss-crossed by a web of roads and dirt tracks.

Luckily, there were no minefields, though Danny spent most of that night trying to extricate himself from the grounds of the military complex which, since the bombing raid, had been filled with patrolling foot soldiers, roaring troop-trucks, and heavily guarded mobile gun batteries.

Eventually, feeling exhausted and in a state of disorientation, he came to a road junction, where he found himself stuck between a three-man vehicle-control point and a fixed AA gun site. Unable to go forward, but determined not to turn back, he crawled into a culvert beneath the road, scraping his already bloody knees and losing more blood.

The culvert was filled with foul-smelling rubbish that almost made him retch. His feet, as well as his raw knees, had become extremely painful, with many cuts and ulcerated blisters. As it was pitch dark in the culvert, he could do little about this and instead, as the night progressed and the silence wrapped itself around him, he was tormented with hunger, thirst and cold.

At first light he moved on, circling around the vehicle-control point and the gun batteries, feeling increasingly weak and dizzy, aware that he was losing his sense of balance and might not last much longer. This, he dimly realized, was due to dehydration, which would kill him if he failed to find water. Miraculously, just as he saw another vehicle-control point and was about to collapse at the mere sight of it, he came across a small stream flowing over white stones of surprising brightness. Filled with gratitude and relief, he dropped to his hands and knees, then shoved his whole face into the freezing water and greedily drank it.

Just as quickly jerking upright with revulsion, he spat the water out. It was foul. Even worse, it was burning his mouth and tongue. Forcing spittle into his mouth to rid himself of the bitter, acid taste, he spat again, though could not stop shivering with weakness, shock and growing nausea. Already, that single, brief taste of the water had scorched and blistered his mouth, making his tongue swell up dangerously, threatening to choke him.

Glancing down into the water, at the surprisingly pure white stones below, he realized they had been burnt clean by the same substance that was searing his mouth. Chemical waste. Recognizing the fact, Danny went into a spasm of repeated vomiting, which only ended when there was nothing left to throw up. Now, with his belly empty and his swollen tongue threatening to choke him, he knew that he was on his last legs and could not last much longer. However, recalling all he had been taught in the Combat and Survival Phase of Continuation Training, he refused to give in to despair and instead crawled into another culvert, where he lay up all day, trying to regain his strength and conquer his hunger and thirst by force of will.

To an extent, he succeeded, and once the darkness fell he walked past the vehicle-control point in dead ground, where he could not be seen. But he was barely past it when flashing in the sky far behind him indicated that the facility was being bombed again by the Allies. This time, he could not have run even if he had had to – though luckily there was no need. The facility was now a long way behind him, with the sounds of the air raid mercifully distant and muffled. Eventually darkness reclaimed the sky and the silence returned.

Danny, though unsteady on his feet, resolutely kept walking. Suddenly, in the dark night, he came upon barbed-wire fencing that appeared to run for miles on both sides of him. Assuming he had reached the border, he climbed over the barbed wire where wooden stakes had been driven through it for support. The pain was excruciating, particularly when the barbed wire tore his already bleeding knees and hands, but he gritted his teeth and endured, sweating profusely, until he could drop down to the other side.

Lights were shining in the distance, but by now he was so weak and confused he was starting to hear voices in his head.

'*It'll be there in the Imperial War Museum for your children to read,*' Andrew said distinctly.

Shocked, Danny glanced about him, but there was no sign of Andrew. Then he remembered that he was marching all alone and that Andrew had either been killed or captured.

'*The men in that mobile unit packed up their plates and saucers this morning,*' Ricketts said, loud and clear, '*and I think they'll be leaving soon.*'

Danny glanced around again, but Ricketts was nowhere in sight.

'*We need a loaf of bread,*' Darlene said. '*Can you go out and get one, luv?*'

'Yes, Darlene,' Danny replied to the bitter wind.

As he walked towards the distant lights, which he hoped were friendly houses, he collapsed twice and each time became unconscious. The second time, he fell flat on his face and saw, when he recovered and examined himself in his hand mirror, that he had broken his formerly perfect nose.

'Very nice,' he said to the mirror. 'Now you look more mature.'

During moments of lucidity, Danny realized that he was in serious trouble and was likely to collapse for good if he did not find drinkable water soon. At first light, badly depleted, afraid that collapse was imminent, he sat with his back against the wall of a wadi and distinctly heard his mates calling to him.

'Hey, Baby Face!' Jock called.

'Quick, Danny!' yelled Paddy. 'Get your arse over here!'

What Danny could see, however, about 200 yards away, was an isolated goatherd's shack. Two hundred yards was not far, but to him it seemed miles.

'Damn it, Danny,' he said aloud, but with difficulty because his tongue was so swollen, 'don't give up now. You've come this far, go the rest of the mile. Stand up, Danny. Start walking.'

That was enough to get him started. It even brought his senses back. He remembered to break down his rifle into its component parts to show that he was not a combatant. Carrying the pieces in a small sack, he managed to walk as far as the goatherd's shack, where he found a woman outside, kneeling by an open fire boiling soup in a pan as children played happily around her. She looked up, unsurprised, when Danny stopped before her and coughed into his clenched fist.

'Hello,' he said in his basic Arabic. 'Sorry to trouble you, but could you tell me exactly where I am?'

Registering from his appearance and imperfect Arabic that he was a Coalition soldier, the woman smiled and waved to the other side of the barbed-wire fence, where Danny saw a border post with an Iraqi flag fluttering on its watch-tower. The woman spoke to him in Arabic, then, seeing that he didn't understand, pointed to the watch-tower and said, 'Iraq!' She then pointed to the ground at her feet and said, 'Syria. *Syria!*'

Realizing that he had made it, after marching for six days and seven nights, and covering a total of 117 miles, Danny raised his hand in a weak gesture of gratitude, then collapsed.

15

Arriving safely in Syria at separate locations and different times, Ricketts and Danny were handed over to the Coalition forces and flown immediately to Tabuk in the northern desert of Saudi Arabia, then from there back to the SAS FOB located 87 miles inside Iraq.

Reunited with a relieved Major Hailsham in his lean-to in the FOB, the three men shared their regrets over the deaths of Geordie and Moorcock, then speculated briefly on what had happened to those gone missing – specifically the much-loved Sergeant Andrew Winston, the lesser known, relatively new troopers Gillett and Stone, and, of course, the redoubtable biker, Trooper Johnny Boy Willoughby, and the American Special Forces Master-Sergeant Red Polanski. Knowing that they were either dead or imprisoned, possibly even being tortured, and that nothing could be done to help them, the three men in the lean-to became embarrassed and hastily changed the subject.

'You might like to know, Danny,' Major Hailsham said, 'that the reason we couldn't respond to your SARBE beacon is that according to Intelligence the Iraqis alerted nearly two thousand troops when you escaped. Those, along with extensive helicopter and aircraft recces, made picking you up, let alone finding you, virtually impossible. In fact, they even alerted civilians along the river-bank to look out for you and any others like you.'

'Yes,' Danny replied, 'I sussed that. That's why I was constantly encountering troops on the move or civilians walking about the whole night, from last to first light. That's why it took me so long.'

'You were lucky you got here at all,' Hailsham said. 'That was a record-breaking march by any standards, and you did it through the heart of enemy territory and came out in one piece. That's some achievement, Corporal.'

'Thanks, boss.'

'And all you suffered was a broken nose,' Ricketts said. 'It makes you look more mature.'

'Thank *you*, Sergeant-Major!'

Ricketts and Hailsham grinned.

'How did you actually get back to safety?' Hailsham asked. 'Some Syrian woman, did you say? Any hanky-panky?'

Danny blushed and looked terribly serious. 'No, boss,' he said. 'I collapsed from exhaustion, hunger and relief when that Syrian woman told me I'd crossed the border. While I was still unconscious, the woman's husband put me on a bed of straw in the barn for the animals. He left me there until I recovered. I slept there until I was ready to leave.'

'Sleeping with the animals,' Hailsham said. 'As close to nature as a man can possibly get. And then?'

'When I regained consciousness, the woman built up my strength with a daily diet of soup and bread. When I was fit enough to walk, she took me to the nearest town, where a fat Syrian official handed me over to the police. When I showed them my letter of reward for safe transfer, they tore it up, threw me in a filthy cell and beat the shit out of me – just for fun, I think.'

'Absolutely disgraceful,' Hailsham said.

'No argument there, boss.'

'And so?'

'Having got that little bit of aggro out of

their systems, they drove me away in a battered Mercedes, passing a sign pointing to Baghdad. When I commented on this, the bastards had another bit of sport by saying that's where they were taking me – to hand me over to Saddam's secret police. Luckily, they were just joking. In fact, they drove me to a Saudi border town, where I was handed over to the British Embassy. The toffs in the Embassy, who seemed embarrassed by my presence, got me on that American plane flying in to Tabuk. I guess you know all the rest.'

'No saucy scandals, then?' Hailsham still looked hopeful.

'Sorry, boss. Can't help you there.'

'We're glad to have you back all the same,' Hailsham said in his most soothing manner. 'You were quite lucky, Danny.'

'Yes, boss, I was.'

'So was I,' Ricketts said. 'A lot luckier than those other poor sods, caught by the Iraqis.'

Realizing, by the sudden silence, that he had got back onto an unwelcome subject, Ricketts glanced out of Hailsham's camouflaged lean-to at the many tanks, trucks, mobile gunnery units, Land Rovers, LSVs and motorbikes spread between the other tents in the setting sun. The sight of them sent a powerful surge of pride through him. Suddenly ashamed, however, of the pleasure he was feeling when the others might be in bad trouble, even dead, he coughed into his fist, returned his gaze to Hailsham, and asked, 'How are things going with the war?'

'It's practically over,' Hailsham said. 'The air strikes have severely damaged Saddam's airfields and disrupted his command and control structure. We've broken his communications links to the front. Ninety per cent of Iraq's internal communications have been knocked out and the transportation of fuel severely disrupted. Damage to ammunition storage dumps has been slight so far, but the long-term supply of missiles has been seriously interrupted and the production of chemical-warfare stocks hit hard. The national electricity grid has been shut down. The Scuds have been pursued into the wilds of Iraq, well out of harm's way – at least out of range of Israel – and our own raids have spread panic and confusion throughout the Iraqi army, which has, according to the green slime, mistaken our small numbers for a regiment of about ten thousand men.'

'And the ground war?'

'It's well under way. Two major invasion forces

crossed the border simultaneously at 0400 hours the day before yesterday. In the east, elements of the 1st and 2nd US Marine Divisions broke through the minefields into Kuwait and fought their way due north towards Kuwait City. At the same time, in the far west, elements of the American 18 Corps, with French reinforcements, made a wide sweep across the desert. The Americans eventually severed Highway 8, which runs from Basra to Baghdad, thereby trapping the Republican Guard divisions. While they were doing that, the French were securing the western flank of the advance.'

'Neat,' Ricketts said.

'The third part of the invasion,' Hailsham continued, 'was the airborne attack by the 101st Assault Division – the Screaming Eagles – who shipped two thousand men in three hundred helicopters to establish an FOB well inside Iraq, striking at the severed Highway 8. Meanwhile, in the east, the US Navy was shelling the coast and the 1st US Cavalry Division were continuing their artillery raids and reconnaissance patrols in the area of Wadi at Batin. By G plus one, the day after the start of the ground war, the British 7th Armoured Brigade, spearheaded by the Queen's Royal Hussars and fourteen hundred Challenger tanks, was advancing into Iraq along the sixteen lanes opened up by the 1st Mechanized Infantry Division. Right now, even as we talk, and while the Iraqis are inexplicably continuing to focus their attention on their southern front, the Americans in the north-west are cutting the highway to Baghdad, the Arab forces in the east are advancing on Kuwait, the Egyptians are taking large numbers of prisoners, and 18 Corps is advancing towards the Republican Guard divisions in the far north-east. Already nearly ten thousand prisoners had been captured and hundreds more are waving white flags. You got back just in time.'

'For what? What are we slated for?'

Before Hailsham could answer, a familiar, insolent voice cracked like a whip: '*Sir*! Trooper John Willoughby reporting for duty, *sir*!'

Looking around in surprise, Ricketts, Danny and Major Hailsham saw Johnny Boy snapping to attention and clipping a theatrically smart salute, even though his beret was missing and his desert clothing covered in blood and filth. He had a broad, cheeky grin on his handsome face.

'Johnny Boy!' Danny cried out in surprise.

'Jesus!' Ricketts murmured.

'Well, I'll be damned,' Hailsham said. 'Please

give me, an explanation, Trooper, for your recent absence.'

''Scuse me, boss,' Johnny Boy said, 'but Trooper Willoughby is absolutely shagged and begs permission to sit.'

'Place your arse on a chair, Trooper Willoughby, then make your report.'

Still grinning cockily, Johnny Boy took one of the folding chairs at the table, wiped some dust off his bloody, filthy clothes, swept his blonde hair back from his forehead with an elegant hand movement, then nodded, as if congratulating himself.

'Well, sir . . .' he began.

'Where's Master-Sergeant Polanski?' Hailsham interjected.

'In the hospital at Riyadh,' the trooper answered, 'waiting to be shipped back to the States. He has a hole in his side and it hurts like hell, but he's going to be OK. Some guy, that old Red!'

'We all knew you adored him,' Hailsham responded drily. 'Now go back to the beginning, dear boy.'

'Yes, boss.' Johnny Boy leant forward comfortably in his seat like a born storyteller. 'Well, boss, when we were following you on the Honda, a mortar shell took us out and we found ourselves

SOLDIER A: SAS

lying on the desert floor with the Iraqis steaming right at us.'

'That's when we lost you,' Hailsham said.

'Yes, boss, that was it. I picked my face out of the sand and saw you racing away . . .'

'Go on,' Hailsham said.

'Well,' Johnny Boy continued, polishing each word like a gem, 'I was pretty bruised from the fall and old Red seemed unconscious, which may be why the Iraqis neither killed us nor beat the shit out of us. Instead, most of them chased you lot while one truck stayed behind to pick us up. I pretended to be unconscious – at least *almost* unconscious – you know? Moaning and groaning with eyes closed – and since Red apparently was that way, they must have thought we were harmless . . .'

'How unimaginative,' Hailsham interjected softly.

'. . . so they threw us into the back of a soft-topped truck, on the floor, surrounded by half a dozen exhausted militiamen.'

Johnny Boy straightened up, drawing out the silence for effect, then beamed and leant forward again to continue his story.

'Of course, we didn't have any weapons. At least that's what the poor sods thought. But I

248

still had my commando knife tucked down my boot and the daft bastards didn't see that. The truck had turned around and was heading back the way it had come when old Red groaned and opened his eyes and then gave me the wink. One of the Iraqis kicked his arse and he groaned again and closed his eyes, acting as if he was half-dead and pretty well out of it. But I knew he wasn't. So, when the Iraqis started gibbering among themselves, having an argument about something, I slipped out my knife and slammed it into the boot right by my hand – right through the guy's foot.'

'Very good,' Hailsham murmured.

'He came off his seat screaming, dropping his Kalashnikov right on top of me, and I grabbed it and was sitting up and firing before the others knew what was happening. I did the six of them and the driver – shot him through the back of the neck. The truck went out of control and raced on across the desert, which conveniently was flat, and finally slowed down of its own accord, then stopped altogether. Old Red helped me throw the stiffs out, including the driver, then I got behind the wheel and we drove off – not after you, in case we ran into the ones following you, but

45 degrees the other way, hoping to circle back towards you.'

'Obviously you didn't make it,' Hailsham said.

Johnny Boy sighed melodramatically. 'No, sir. We drove for about two hours and then – would you believe it? – we were attacked by an American F-15E, using Sidewinder missiles and cannon fire. We dived out of the truck just before it was hit, but Polanski didn't manage to run away as fast as me and so received a piece of flying debris in his gut when the truck blew apart.'

'He's *older* than you,' Hailsham remarked.

'Yes, boss, that's true.'

'We must practise humility,' Hailsham told him. 'So what happened next?'

'That piece of burning-hot, sharp metal punched a hole right though him, just missing his stomach, though still losing him an awful lot of blood.' The trooper shook his head in disbelieving recollection. 'Can you guess what old John Wayne did then?'

'I'm sure you'll inform us,' Rickett said.

'With no more than a field dressing and morphine to keep him going, he walked with me for two days and nights, constantly cursing his wound but not letting it bring him down, and

250

boasting that this was the kind of A1 endurance number that only the supermen of his Yankee Delta Force could pull off.'

'I can imagine,' Hailsham said wearily.

'Then, on the third day,' Johnny Boy went on, oblivious to Hailsham's gentle irony, 'we came across an Iraqi border post, near Saudi Arabia. It only had a few guards inside and one truck outside. Having taken a couple of hand-grenades off the Iraqis I'd killed, I sneaked up on the border post at last light, mailed them a couple of grenades in through the window, and ran like hell back to where Red, though still bleeding profusely, was keeping me covered with the Kalashnikov we'd stolen from the Iraqis who'd captured us. The border post went up in smoke and all the guards inside were killed. We took the truck parked near the gate and drove to the border. When we got there, we ditched the truck and weapons and crossed over on foot, with old Red, now bleeding worse than ever, not stopping once. We found ourselves in Scud Boulevard and the Yanks – some guys from Red's Delta Force – came out of nowhere to pick us up. They choppered us back to Riyadh, rushed Red to the medics, and shoved me onto a passing Chinook to get me back here. So here I am, boss.'

The trooper sat back in his chair and beamed at them all. However, the praise he was so clearly expecting failed to materialize.

'About bloody time,' Hailsham said instead. 'Now let's get back to business.'

While Johnny Boy was looking distinctly hard done by, Hailsham, trying to hide his grin, turned back to Ricketts.

'As I was saying, Sergeant-Major, we're going back into Iraq. While the advance is continuing, there's still lots for us to do – espionage, ambush, disruption, confusion, and general hit-and-run raids against communications towers and the remaining Scuds. We won't be short of work.'

'Where is it this time?' Ricketts asked.

'We're going back to Scud Alley.'

16

For the next five days, as the war wound down to a close, Hailsham's men roamed and struck with growing confidence at an enemy increasingly demoralized. Their favourite hunting ground was Wadi Amiq, also known as Wadi Amij, running west between two main roads from the Euphrates to the town of Ar Rutbah – part of the area known as Scud Alley.

Having no specific targets, but determined to cause as much disruption and confusion as possible with hit-and-run raids on anything crossing their path, the men spent the first day roaming the terrain with the aid of their Magellan satellite navigation systems, prepared to take on anything they could find.

They found nothing at all. On the second day, however, when cruising across the desert at noon, they spotted a mobile Iraqi convoy of fourteen

253

vehicles, including Scud transporter-erectors and escorts for defence against attack by tanks and aircraft. Parked alongside the trail, the convoy was under camouflage, but clearly preparing to move off again. As it did so, Hailsham followed, calling an air strike while on the move.

Thirty minutes later four F-15s arrived to attack the column one after another with Sidewinder missiles. As usual, the explosions were spectacularly ferocious, creating great mushrooms of spiralling sand and flying debris of all kinds. But when the sand had settled down it was clear that only one of the four strikes had hit the target, leaving a solitary transporter-erector in ruins in an immense, blackened shell hole. When the four strike aircraft flew off to return to base, the rest of the Iraqi column remained untouched.

'Bloody Air Force!' Johnny Boy said in disgust. 'They couldn't hit a barn door if you took them by the hand and led them up to it.'

'The wonders of technology,' Ricketts added. 'We didn't paint the targets with our designators and there's the sorry result – practically nothing.'

'It's back to good, old-fashioned ground warfare,' Hailsham said. 'Let's try the MILANs.'

With the LSVs bringing up the rear, Hailsham led his Pink Panther Land Rovers forward to a location within range, and within sight, of the enemy column. There the men quickly uncovered their MILAN anti-tank guided missile units, one to each Pink Panther. At 765mm in length, weighing 27.68kg, and with a bulky launcher-guidance unit, periscopic optical sight, missile tube with folding wings, wide exit point for 6.66kg shells, and an exceptionally sturdy tripod, the MILAN was an impressive piece of equipment to have mounted on the back of a Land Rover.

Experts one and all, the troopers in the Pink Panthers picked separate targets in the column, then aimed and fired almost simultaneously. The sound of the combined backblasts was impressive, with smoke spewing from both ends of the MILANs. Less than ten seconds later an Iraqi transporter-erector and three trucks exploded, virtually at the same time.

'So much for the Air Force!' Danny said, glancing at Ricketts and offering a rare smile. 'Let the bastards beat that!'

But even before the smoke of the explosions had cleared, the Iraqi triple-A machine guns mounted on wheeled transports hit back with a continuous barrage of fire, causing bullets to ricochet off the Pink Panthers with a harsh metallic drumming while the sand was stitched in jagged lines about them.

Realizing that he was outgunned, Hailsham ordered the Pink Panthers to make a tactical withdrawal, out of range of the Iraqi machine-guns. Then he called on US air power again.

This time, when the F-15s swept down, they struck more accurately, making strikes along most of the column, causing the few remaining trucks and one transporter-erector to race away from billowing black smoke and flames toward the sun-streaked horizon.

While heading back to base, Hailsham's column was attacked by an A-10 pilot who obviously mistook the Land Rovers and LSVs, moving almost bumper to bumper, for a single long Iraqi vehicle, perhaps a mobile Scud launcher. Coming in low, the pilot raked the column with his cannons, causing two of the Land Rovers to explode while the others scattered quickly, churning up clouds of sand, to avoid suffering a similar fate.

'Stupid bloody Air Force!' Johnny Boy exploded, shaking his free fist at the departing aircraft as he roared past Captain Hailsham's Land Rover on his green Honda. 'Are you all fucking blind?'

'I don't blame him,' Captain Hailsham said,

standing up in his Pink Panther and clearing the sand from his eyes with a delicate, probing finger. 'I'm beginning to wonder myself. OK, driver, take us back to the others.'

Regrouping after the attack, the men in the remaining vehicles were relieved to find that the occupants of the two damaged Pink Panthers had managed to jump out before their petrol tanks exploded. Dividing the men among the remaining vehicles, they left the damaged Land Rovers smouldering in the sand and headed back across the barren desert.

Less than an hour later they came over a low hill to find themselves facing a heavily defended Iraqi observation tower. They had barely seen it when a barrage of gunfire from a whole troop of Iraqi militiamen caused them to urgently spread out in different directions and circle back to the top of the ridge, which gave some protection.

While some of them jumped out of the vehicles to give covering fire from behind the Pink Panthers, others put down a heavy barrage with the vehicles' 7.62 GPMGs or rear-mounted 0.5in Browning heavy machine-guns.

Even from where he was kneeling at the back of a Pink Panther, leaning out repeatedly to fire his SLR, Ricketts could see the sand boiling around the Iraqis as the rapid fire of the machine-guns tore at the ground around them, between them and below them. Some of them fell over, cut down by the hail of bullets, but the others, clearly seasoned troopers, merely slipped back into the shadow of the observation tower and released another barrage of gunfire from there.

This caused sand to spew up around the SAS men, as well as ricocheting dangerously off the Pink Panthers and LSVs.

'If those bastards hit my bike,' Johnny Boy said, obviously frustrated at not being able to do much other than hide behind the Pink Panther, 'I think I'll go apeshit.'

'Those Iraqis are well hidden in the shadows of that tower,' Ricketts said, 'while we're out here in the open like sitting ducks. I say we stop worrying about the militiamen and take the tower out instead.'

'Good thinking,' Hailsham replied. Twisting around to glance back along the line of Pink Panthers, he said: 'Go down the line, Willoughby, and tell the men with the LAWs and mortars to keep striking at the base of that tower. I want them to bring it down.'

'Yes, boss,' the trooper said with a cocky schoolboy's grin. 'I'm on my way, boss.'

'You stay here,' Ricketts said. 'I'll go instead. I want to make sure they do this properly. OK, boss?'

'Fine,' Hailsham said.

'Can't I come with you?' Johnny Boy begged.

'OK,' Ricketts said. He crawled down the line until he reached the Pink Panthers run by the team with the 60mm light anti-tank weapon, or LAW – a single-shot rocket firing a 66mm warhead capable of penetrating tanks and aircraft at 300 metres. When he told the LAW team what he wanted, one of them removed the protective caps from each end of the launcher, then extended the tube containing the rocket to its full length of 90cm. The folding sight popped up automatically. The second man held the launcher on his shoulder and looked along the sight. Ricketts gave him the target, but told him to wait for his signal. He then crawled over to the mortar team crouched behind the adjoining Pink Panther.

The L16 ML 81mm mortar has an adjustable bipod supporting the tube that holds the sighting mechanism. With a range of over five kilometres, it is usually fired at a target identified by a forward observer; but in this case the compass bearing would be ignored in favour of guesswork, using the calibrated dial sight for aiming. When

Ricketts told the mortar team what he wanted, one of the men adjusted the bipod to give the nearest correct angle for the estimated range, then waited for Ricketts to signal.

Having given both teams estimated measurements for the two front supports of the observation tower, where sand was still spitting wildly from the relentless SAS fire, Ricketts raised and then lowered his right hand.

The LAW and the mortar fired at the same time. After a few seconds – though it seemed longer than that – two simultaneous explosions erupted on either side of the base of the tower, just missing it, but killing some of the Iraqi soldiers firing out of its shadow.

'Fuck,' one of the LAW team said. 'Too short.'

'Not by much,' his partner said. 'We just need about five more degrees elevation and we should hit it right on the nose.'

'Go to it,' Ricketts said. 'When you get the proper range and actually hit the base of the tower, keep shelling the exact same spot until you blow it away. If the mortar team does the same to the other side, the whole caboose should fall down.'

'Right on top of those fucking militiamen,' Johnny Boy enthused.

'You've got it,' Ricketts replied.

The Iraqi response to the shelling was an extended burst of machine-gun fire from the observation post on top of the tower and a more violent barrage from the militiamen hidden in the shadows beneath it. Safe behind their Pink Panthers, the LAW and mortar teams reloaded their weapons, raised the elevation a few degrees, and fired off another simultaneous round. This time the explosions appeared to be right on target, but when the swirling smoke and spewing sand finally cleared away, it was evident that the shells had again fallen short, though dispatching more militiamen in the process.

'Third time lucky,' one of the LAW men said.

'No question, mate,' his partner replied.

They were correct. The third set of simultaneous explosions erupted right under the crisscrossing steel supports of the tower, blackening and buckling them slightly, as well as killing more Iraqi troops.

'That's it,' Ricketts said. 'You're dead on target. Now keep pouring those shells on exactly the same spot and you should be able to bring that bastard down.'

'It's as good as done,' the LAW man said.

Though the Iraqis were still managing to keep

up enough fire-power to cause devastation to the ground around the SAS troop, with bullets ricocheting off the vehicles and making the sand explode in jagged, snake-like lines about them, the repeated shelling by the LAW and 81mm mortar, combined with the relentless small-arms fire of the rest of the squadron, soon turned the base of the observation tower into an inferno of spitting, swirling sand and smoke. That the Iraqis still managed to return the fire at all was amazing, since it seemed they must surely choke to death, if not actually dying in the hail of bullets. Yet they did courageously return the fire, albeit with diminishing ferocity, while the supports of the tower behind them buckled more with each explosion, smouldered, turned blacker, and the structure itself began to tilt forward at a dangerous angle.

Though the machine-gunner high up in the observation post kept firing, some of the observers started clambering down the ladder, clearly frightened that the tower was going to topple.

It did so before any of the fleeing men reached the ground. As two final explosions smashed through the buckled lower supports, the tower tilted forward still further, the ladder snapped free and the men scrambling down it screamed as they fell off and plunged up to fifty feet to the ground. The tower was now leaning even more, with its support girders buckling and breaking, and the militiamen on the ground started running as it finally crashed down.

With the Iraqi troops on the ground coming out into the open, many were either killed in the withering hail of fire from the SAS or died when the enormous tower crushed them under tons of crumpling, shrieking metal. Its collapse shook the desert floor and created a mushroom cloud of sand that obscured the men screaming and dying in a tangle of steel.

Even before the spiralling sand had subsided, Johnny Boy was back on his Honda, driving with one hand, brandishing his Browning pistol in the other, leading the Pink Panthers and LSVs towards the few Iraqis who had miraculously escaped and were trying to take cover behind the wreckage. The trooper ignored the bullets whining past his head, though he weaved left and right to make himself more difficult to hit and eventually swept out and in again, coming up behind his victims to pick them off one by one as he roared past.

Meanwhile the Pink Panthers and LSVs continued advancing from the front, but spread out to form two semicircles that encompassed the wreckage. The men fired on the move, keeping up a relentless barrage, not stopping until the handful of remaining Iraqis, now dazed and terrified, threw down their weapons and waved their *shemaghs* like flags, in surrender.

Captain Hailsham used a hand signal to indicate 'Cease fire'.

The sudden silence was eerie, as was the sight of the surviving militiamen raising their hands in the ruins, ghostlike in the swirling dust and smoke, covered in dust themselves, surrounded by a multitude of dead, some shot, others crushed by the girders, which, now littering the desert floor and obscured by drifting dust, formed an immense, hideous sarcophagus of steel.

After accepting the surrender of the ten surviving Iraqis, Hailsham divided them between the Pink Panthers and drove them back to base, where a soft-topped truck with armed escort drove them on to the FOB. From there they would be taken to one of the growing number of Allied POW camps.

Having disposed of the prisoners, Hailsham let his men have a good night's rest, then led

them back into the desert for another day of
hit-and-run raids.

Locating another, less heavily defended Iraqi
observation post, they engaged in another fire-
fight, killing two Iraqis and taking half a dozen
prisoners. That was Day Two.

During Day Three they called in an air strike
against a large radar complex built around a
microwave communications tower. The complex
was pulverized and the tower collapsed into the
dust, leaving nothing but debris on the smoke-
wreathed plain and another bunch of prisoners
to be looked after.

On Day Four, as the increasingly successful
column of Pink Panthers and LSVs made its way
back toward the Saudi border, they were attacked
by another troop of Iraqis. This time, however,
the Iraqis had the advantage, being strung out
along, and partially hidden by, an irregular ridge
that blocked the path of the SAS column.

The ambush opened with simultaneous mortar
explosions that tore up the ground between the
Pink Panthers and LSVs. One of the latter was
picked up by an explosion and slewed to the
side, cutting a groove through the ground and
hurling up sand behind it, before rolling over
and coming to rest upside down, throwing its

occupants clear. One of the unfortunate crew remained where he was lying, limbs akimbo, splashed with blood, but the other stood up and was immediately flung onto his back by a savage burst of machine-gun fire.

Even as the shot trooper spasmed violently and died, the other SAS vehicles were breaking off in opposite directions, weaving between the explosions and the spitting, bullet-riddled sand, to circle back and form a defensive laager further away from the ridge. Once in semicircular formation, the men jumped out of the vehicles, taking cover behind them, in some instances dragging down the heavy GPMGs in order to mount them on tripods on the desert floor and give the Iraqis as good as they were getting.

'Get those mortars set up!' Hailsham bawled, practically rolling backwards out of his Pink Panther to fall to the sand and pick himself up again. 'I want that whole ridge blown to hell. Corporal Clarke,' he said to Paddy, who was already firing his SLR, 'I want you to take some men and bug out south of here, then circle west and come back under cover of that slight incline to our right to do as much damage as you can manage from that angle. Take a GPMG.'

'Right, boss,' Paddy said.

The ground roared and erupted at the other side of the Pink Panther, showering Hailsham and those around him.

'Corporal McGregor,' Hailsham called to Jock, who was firing bursts from his M16, 'I want you to do the same, but circle east until you're parallel with Paddy. I want your team to take a GPMG as well.'

'Right, boss. Will do.'

'Get going, then.' As Paddy and Jock crawled away, trying to avoid the spitting bullets and mortar explosions, Hailsham glanced at Danny, also firing his SLR, then turned to Ricketts, saying, 'Well, we certainly walked into this one. How on earth do we get out?'

Casting his gaze beyond the overturned LSV and the two lifeless SAS troopers spread-eagled near it, Ricketts saw that the irregular ridge was rendering the Iraqis practically invisible. Their mortars were set up slightly down the slope behind the ridge and most of the men using small arms were lying behind the ledge of the rim, only raising their heads above it long enough to fire and duck down again. It was indeed possible that Jock and Paddy would be able to pick some off from the side, but most of them would still be out of sight, firing with impunity unless taken out by SAS mortars.

As if to help Hailsham and Ricketts with their sombre deliberations, the SAS mortar teams started firing from just behind them, lobbing their shells high in order to let them fall behind the ridge. This they did, churning up spirals of sand that rose above the ridge, hopefully signifying that damage had been inflicted on the Iraqis, though that could not be verified.

Ricketts glanced east and west to see Jock and Paddy, each trailing a three-man team and GPMG, circling around from far behind to come up on either side of the laager and lay down a two-pronged barrage.

'I can't see us going forward,' Ricketts said, 'because there's no way of advancing up that ridge without insupportable losses.'

'I agree,' Hailsham said. 'On the other hand, if we head back the way we came, they'll just up roots and follow us. By then, we'll be deep in their territory and ripe for the picking.'

'Call in an air strike,' Danny suggested, 'and let them do the work for us.'

'We're too close,' Hailsham told him. 'Any air strike is going to strike us, so let's leave them out of it.'

'We can go back further,' Danny said.

'They'll pick us off like flies,' Ricketts reminded him, 'the minute we climb up into the dinkies.'

'Which gets us back where we started,' Hailsham said. 'Right here. Still trapped.'

At that moment, the GPMG of Jock's team started roaring, the bullets making the sand dance in a jagged line that first exploded just below the ridge and then followed an erratic, oblique course up to its rim, where the bullets whined off harmlessly into thin air.

Less than a minute later the other GPMG did the same, with similar results. Both teams were rewarded when mortar shells from somewhere behind the ridge whistled down and exploded dangerously close to them, showering the men and their useless GPMGs with sand, soil and gravel.

Shortly after those mortar shells had been followed by others, coming closer all the time, Jock used his PRC 319 to contact Hailsham and inform him that he still could not see a thing beyond the ridge, even though he was clearly a sitting duck for the Iraqi mortar teams behind it.

When Paddy called in with the same message, Hailsham told both teams to bug out.

At that moment an Iraqi mortar shell hit a Pink Panther, filling the air with flying debris that caused almost as much damage as the blast itself. When the smoke had cleared away and those nearby had regained their hearing – namely, Hailsham, Ricketts and Danny – they saw one SAS trooper pinned lifeless beneath the smouldering remains of the vehicle, another lying in a pool of blood with his neck almost severed by a piece of jagged metal, and a third, though still alive, badly peppered by shrapnel and groaning, semi-conscious, in terrible pain.

'Let's *all* bug out,' Captain Hailsham said. 'We have no other option. We'll shoot and scoot, and hope for the best. After that, it's each man for himself. What do you say?'

'Shoot and scoot,' Ricketts confirmed.

'Have that wounded man picked up and placed in my Pink Panther,' Hailsham told Danny. 'Then pass the word around the laager that we're going to shoot and scoot, meeting back at the FOB in our own time. We go at my signal.'

'Right, boss,' Danny said. He scurried off at the crouch as more mortar shells exploded, showering all of them yet again.

Glancing in both directions, Ricketts saw Jock and Paddy coming back in with their teams, crouched low and weaving, with the ground erupting behind them and sand spitting viciously between them. Miraculously, they all managed to get back into the laager without being hit.

Just as they arrived back, two troopers heaved the wounded man, now on a makeshift stretcher, up into the rear of Hailsham's Pink Panther and Danny took his place in the adjoining vehicle, preparing to drive Ricketts out.

Johnny Boy was swinging his leg over the Honda and already revving it up.

'Fucking A,' he said. 'Right!'

Captain Hailsham raised his hand high in the air, held it there for a moment, then dropped it, bawling: '*Shoot and scoot!*'

The Pink Panthers and LSVs roared into life, revving up, as Johnny Boy shot ahead in a cloud of churning sand, this time gripping the handlebars firmly. Racing up towards the ridge with Iraqi bullets whining about him, he was followed almost instantly by the Pink Panthers and LSVs, their troopers already firing at the ridge with their small arms and GPMGs. The crest of the ridge was torn apart by the syncopated barrage of gunfire.

Suddenly Johnny Boy sailed into the air, leaving behind his motorbike, which exploded in mid-air, and flinging his arms wide as he somersaulted and crashed back down again.

He was dead and they all knew it, so no one stopped for him. Instead they swerved around him and raced on up the slope to reach the top of the ridge, mangle some stunned Iraqis, then bounce and swerve down the other side in dense clouds of swirling sand.

One LSV hit the ground nose-first. It somersaulted and crashed, throwing one trooper out, crushing the other, and exploding when its fuel tank burst and bullets set it on fire. The trooper flung clear, as he was peppered by Iraqi bullets, was mercifully already dead from a broken neck.

The rest raced down the other side, bursting out of the trap, and then spread out, heading off in different directions, to confuse the Iraqis.

Captain Hailsham saw the wide open spaces and could hardly believe it. Ricketts saw the same – the vast sweep of the empty desert – but then he heard a dreadful roaring, felt the hot breath of the beast, and was picked up and hurled through a shocking, unreal, searing silence.

He returned to a recognizable world of clamour and pain.

The sky was above him, mortar shells were

exploding around him, and Danny, whose perfect features had earlier been marred by a broken nose, was leaning over him and trying to talk to him through a roaring shower of earth.

'. . . OK?' Danny bawled.

Ricketts shook his head. He had meant to say 'No' but he couldn't speak.

'Can you get up?' Danny asked.

'No,' Ricketts managed to croak, suddenly visualizing his wife and two daughters back in England, and swelling up with love for them. 'Don't think I can move at all.'

'Shit,' Danny said. Another shell exploded nearby. Bullets were making the sand spit all around him as his eyes filled with tears. 'Damn it, Ricketts, just . . .'

'What happened, Danny?'

'A mortar shell fell too close. We were tipped over, Ricketts, flung out, just before we got clear away.'

'The others?'

'Most of them made it, but they're long gone by now.'

'Get going, Danny. No need to stay with me.'

'The Pink Panther's fit for the wrecker's yard. I'm trapped here with you, boss.'

273

'Start running.'

'No.'

'That's an order.'

'I can't hear it.'

'I thought you were a tough nut, a killer – so why don't you run?'

'Go fuck yourself, Ricketts.' Danny glanced back over his shoulder, up the slope, towards the ridge, and saw a bunch of Iraqis coming down, their weapons aimed at him. 'Too late,' he said, turning back to Ricketts. 'They're calling our number right now and you know what they'll do, boss.'

He reached down, removed his Browning from its holster, held Ricketts's head up, then put the barrel of the gun to his temple.

'You *know* what they'll do, boss. There's no Geneva Convention here. Say the word and I'll finish it. It'll be a lot quicker.'

Ricketts, though still in bad pain, grinned wryly at Danny's suggestion. 'No,' he replied, prepared to get a bullet in the head in combat but not about to invite it in the ritual all SAS wives dreaded. 'I'm not joining the Exit Club just yet. Now get up and run, Danny.'

Danny sighed and turned away from Ricketts

to aim his handgun at the Iraqis. 'No, Sergeant-Major. I've never run in my life. Let's see who gets the most. Start counting, boss.'

'You mad bastard,' Ricketts said.

The Iraqis all fired at once. Ricketts raised his head as the ground erupted around Danny. The baby-faced corporal convulsed, his clothing torn to shreds, blood bursting from bullet holes, and then was picked up and punched back by the fusillade of gunfire, to land with a thud close to Ricketts.

'Danny!' Ricketts screamed. He managed to roll over and touch his friend's shoulder just before the enemy gunfire reached him too, brutally, irrevocably blotting out his whole world.

17

On 26 February 1991, a mere hundred hours after the land war had begun, but nearly seven months after the start of the Iraqi invasion, a defeated Iraq announced that it was withdrawing from Kuwait. Within hours, in a Baghdad Radio broadcast, Saddam Hussein renounced his claims on that country. Subsequently, Allied Marines entered Kuwait City in the wake of the victorious Kuwaiti and Saudi armies.

The capital had already been infiltrated by the Boat Group of the SAS, which had been tasked with spreading confusion and chaos among the Iraqi troops based there. Working closely with the US Navy's SEALS on a programme of disinformation, the SBS had managed to convince the Iraqis that the US Marines were poised to storm the city's shoreline. It had also sabotaged Iraqi bases and set up OPs to call in air strikes and gunfire from the Allied battleships anchored in the Gulf.

Last but not least, it was SAS troops who had captured the British Embassy in Kuwait in the final hours of the war. They abseiled onto the roof from a Sea King helicopter used explosives to blow off the doors, cleared the rooms with stun grenades, and checked that the building was free of booby-traps. Ambassador Michael Weston was then able to return and replace the tattered Union Jack with a new one.

Even after the loss of the badly wounded Sergeant-Major Ricketts, already on his way back to Hereford, Major Hailsham had insisted that his remaining men should be allowed to fight all the way back to Kuwait. During that long march they did little fighting, but instead found themselves collecting more and more Iraqi prisoners, most of whom were in pitiful condition and all too keen to surrender by advancing with hands raised or even lying belly-down in the sand and waiting to be picked up. By that stage, the Allied camps for Iraqi prisoners were growing bigger every day and being looked after by the infantry battalions of the Coldstream Guards, the Royal Highland Fusiliers and the King's Own Scottish Borderers. Passing them in his Pink

Panther, now battered and filthy, Hailsham was reminded of grainy old newsreels of the packed POW camps in Europe during World War Two. Though the most high-tech war in history had just been fought, some things never changed.

Like many of the liberators, Major Hailsham, meeting up with some of his other SAS troops in liberated Kuwait, was shocked by what he found there. As Saddam Hussein had ordered his retreating troops to blow up the city's landmarks, most of its most beautiful and important buildings, including the Emir's residence, the Dasman Palace, were either in ruins or seriously damaged. The beaches and streets of the city were cluttered with munitions that continued to take the lives of many innocent children. A grisly search of the city's morgues, basements and houses used by the Iraqi forces turned up hideous evidence of the widespread use of torture against Kuwaiti citizens, including electrocution and mutilation.

Heightening the hellish atmosphere, the pall of smoke that covered the city had turned the sky a nightmarish, constant black, rendered even more frightening by the oily smoke pouring in from the six hundred or so oil wells cruelly set ablaze by the Iraqis. All around Kuwait City, under that stark black sky, the burning oil wells had created a fearsome wall of fire.

After Saddam's generals officially surrendered in a tent in the sand, the Iraqis started handing over Coalition POWs. While the captured British, American, Saudi and Kuwaiti airmen were welcomed off a Red Cross plane at Riyadh amid a blaze of media attention, two SAS men, troopers Stone and Gillett – the former wounded, the latter badly bruised – were quietly led away from the aircraft by the rear cargo door.

Some hours later, ten other prisoners, including the British Tornado pilot John Peters, who had been paraded so shamelessly on television by the Iraqis shortly after being captured, were also released.

While the widely publicized Peters was shaking hands with British diplomats at the Jordanian border, another man released with him was spirited away from the scene as if he had never existed. That man was SAS Sergeant Andrew Winston.

How did you manage to stay sane in captivity?' Andrew was asked by Major Hailsham when safely back in the barracks in Hereford, England, and having a booze-up in the Paludrine Club with

Hailsham, Jock, Paddy and the recently blooded
troopers Stone and Gillett, both of whom, like
Andrew, had survived their period of brutal
captivity.

Though every man present in the bar was fully
aware of the fact that the SAS had suffered
dreadful losses in Iraq, it was a Regimental
tradition not to discuss the dead, or those who
had failed to 'beat the clock', and so the names
of their own deceased – Sergeant-Major Phil
Ricketts, Sergeant Danny Porter and Trooper
John Willoughby – while on everyone's mind,
had not actually been mentioned.

The names of those who had died had already
been inscribed on plaques fixed to the base of the
Regimental clock tower, at the SAS HQ, Stirling
Lines. Tribute had thus been paid, and now
everyone in the bar was determined to return
to his normal, self-protective routine of bullshit
and banter.

'How did I stay sane?' Andrew repeated mock-
ingly, determined to make light of his heavy
burden as he waved his lined notebook. 'Piece
of piss. I just created some poems in my head,
based on my experiences with my captors, then
wrote them down in this little book on the plane
coming back. That's what kept *me* sane, boss.'

'More bullshit,' Paddy said.

'More hot air,' Jock added.

'We'll have to compare notes,' Stone suggested in his dry, ironic way.

'I didn't know you wrote poetry,' Gillett said. 'Gee, that's really surprised me. When can we read them?'

'Ah, those,' big Andrew replied, flashing his perfect teeth in a teasing smile and doing a neat, theatrical double-take, 'they're tales for another day.'